PREPARE THY WORK

Prepare thy work without,
and make it fit for thyself in the field;
and afterwards build thine house.
Proverbs 24:27

PREPARE THY WORK

Preparing Young Men for Christian Marriage

by Daniel Forster

Doorposts
5905 SW Lookingglass Dr., Gaston, OR 97119

Doorposts
5905 SW Lookingglass Dr
Gaston, OR 97119
www.doorposts.net

To my Future Wife,
with my prayer that one day,
by our Master's grace,
we will stand before Him together
and hear Him say,
"Well done, good and faithful servants;
enter into the joy of thy Lord."

THANK YOU!

My thanks to all who gave generously of your time and advice while helping me with this book. It never would have happened without you!

Vance Adams
Zack Armstrong
Frank Bernard
Scott Chapman
Jeff Cone
Doug & Nora Conser
John Conser
Eli Evans
Howard & Juanita Frazier
Elder Doug Hayes
Rod Jantzen
Michael Lortz
Matt Lyons
Isaac Mahar
Mike & Connie Meyerdierk
Tim Murray
Roger Payne
John Pontier
Tim Roach
Elder Dennis Tuuri
John Unger
Roger Walker
Elder Chris Wilson

Thank you to my family — John, Pam, Joseph, Benjamin, Johanna, Bethany and Susannah, for helping with office jobs and driving mail to town so I could write, for giving helpful input, for bringing me goodies while I wrote, and for your continual encouragement!

Special thanks to my Mama, Pam Forster, for teaching me to write, for suggesting this project, for reading numerous drafts, and for being a constant encouragement to me.

Most of all, my thanks to our faithful God, for giving me life, salvation, and the great blessings of Christian family, church, and friends.

CONTENTS

FOREWORD

by Pam Forster

The idea for this book was born when a young man in our church and his new bride shared the story of their courtship with our church family. I can't recall all the details, but I remember that the young husband described the many emails and phone conversations that had taken place with his future father-in-law. Daniel's good friend was joking with him after the meeting. With his characteristic blend of discernment and humor, Bryan laughed and suggested that the guys should get their act together and start studying so they would be prepared when the right lady came along!

That suggestion got the creative wheels turning in our household! How should parents prepare their sons for courtship and marriage? Surely there was a place for a book that encouraged young men to vigorously apply themselves to gaining wisdom in their single years! What a great project for Daniel, our oldest son, to work on as he sought to wisely use the years of young manhood for God's glory!

It took awhile to convince Daniel that, with God's help and a lot of counsel from other men, he could complete a project like this. But, being the teachable son that he is, he accepted our challenge.

He met with many men, some older and some just recently married, asking questions and seeking counsel. He studied his Bible and read books and talked with us and listened to tapes. He organized and wrote and rewrote. He gave manuscripts to older men and revised his work again to incorporate their suggestions and counsel.

Then, in the middle of all his research and writing, Daniel was given the privilege of witnessing and learning from a real-life courtship in our own household! Our family's concept of courtship has been put into action as our daughter prepares to marry a fine young man who lived out the principles of this book before Daniel ever wrote it.

The result is a book that is written, not by an "expert," but by an eager young man who desires with all his heart to please His Lord in all that he does. After three years of work, Daniel is now a much wiser and more mature young man who can humbly offer this book to other young men and their parents, with the prayer that his labors will bear fruit for Christ's kingdom.

Parents, lead your sons through this book. These are the **only** years you have to prepare your son for courtship and marriage!

Young men, prayerfully work your way through this book, and prepare those "fields" that God has placed you in right now. And then be ready to "build your house."

INTRODUCTION

James had been tense all day. Today, he felt somewhat relieved just to finally get out of the office; it had been so hard for him to focus his mind on work.

As he entered the restaurant, he looked for a suitable place to sit. He chose a booth in one corner of the restaurant and sat down on the wooden bench. For many years of study and hard work, James had been anticipating this meeting, and now it was about to happen!

It had been over a year since the Carter family had joined the church that James attended, and, in getting to know the Carters, James and his parents could see that their family and the Carters shared the same Christian vision. The families enjoyed their visits together, and as they came to know each other better, both families discovered that they shared a similar lifestyle and had many convictions in common.

James had only been waiting for about five minutes when he looked up to see Mr. Carter enter the restaurant. As he approached the table where James sat, James stood up, and the two men greeted each other warmly with a handshake. "Hello, Mr. Carter. I appreciate you taking the time to meet me this evening," said James.

"My pleasure," said Mr. Carter. "Thank you for the invitation. My family enjoyed visiting with yours last Sunday."

"It was great to have you out at our place, Mr. Carter. I know my family had a good time as well."

"I have to just dive in and get right to the subject," thought James. As they both sat down, he said, "Mr. Carter, you're probably wondering why I asked you out to dinner tonight."

"I have been thinking about it, James, but go on – why is it?"

"Well, I have been blessed by getting to know you and your family since we came to this church. It seems like our families share many similar convictions and beliefs, and your family has been a great encouragement to mine as we've come to know each other better."

"I'm glad to hear that our family has been an encouragement to yours," answered Mr. Carter. "We too have enjoyed the growing friendship with your family."

"As you know, I have just recently finished my college studies, and my apprenticeship with my father is nearly finished. I will soon be working with him full-time, without the added obligations of college classes and tests. As I have worked and studied over the past six years, I have done my best to focus on these goals and prepare myself for the future wife and family that I pray God has planned for me."

"Interesting..." thought Mr. Carter.

"As my apprenticeship nears completion, I have been increasingly seeking counsel from my parents and praying for God's direction regarding a future wife. With my parents' approval, I requested our meeting this evening for the purpose of asking you and Mrs. Carter to prayerfully consider me as a potential husband for your daughter Elizabeth. I greatly admire her character, her personality, and her devotion to Jesus, and she is exactly the kind of young lady I have been praying God would provide for me as a wife. At this point, I am asking you and your family to pray and consider whether this might be God's will for Elizabeth. I would be most honored if you would allow me the privilege of courting her with the intention of marriage." James breathed an inner sigh of relief. *"There – I said it,"* he thought to himself.

"I thought this might be what he wanted to talk about," Mr. Carter reflected, thinking back to a conversation he and his wife had held the evening after James had asked him out to dinner. They had considered this as one of the possible reasons for the meeting.

"I'm honored by your request, James," he said. "I'm willing to consider the possibility that you may be the young man God has prepared for my daughter. Of course, I'll need to discuss this and pray about it with my wife and then with Elizabeth."

"Thank you," said James, "I am honored that you would consider me."

"From what I can see, James, you are nearly prepared for marriage, at least in your vocation. Before I mention your interest to my daughter however, I would like to get to know you a little better and ask you some questions. Would you be willing to meet with me a few times next week during my lunch break?"

A Word to Young Men

Can you imagine being the young man in this story? What would you say? Are you ready? Are you spending your time wisely, so that some day, like James, you will be ready?

> *Prepare thy work without, and make it fit for thyself in the field; and afterwards build thine house. (Prov. 24:27)*

This verse was written to you, young man! The truth of this verse may apply to you more right now than at any other time in your life. God has made man to excercise dominion on the earth for His glory, and He has commanded us to be fruitful and multiply. For most men, this will involve receiving God's gift of marriage. The desire to get married and lead a family in faithfulness to God is a good desire, but before we get to that stage in our lives, there is much preparing to be done. Besides establishing a vocation that will provide for a family, we need to be growing in wisdom, in godly manhood, and in our relationship with Jesus. God wants us to know His ways and trust in Him *from our youth* (Ps. 71:5).

If we neglect these pursuits during their proper season, we will reach harvest time and have nothing to harvest! Just like the farmer in this verse, we must plan ahead, prepare our fields, and sow seed today, so that we will be ready to build our house later. Like the farmer, we need to faithfully tend the fields we've been entrusted with *right now*, so that we will be ready to support and lead our households later in life. The "house" that Proverbs 24:27 refers to is not just a structure, but also our very family and future descendants. This word for "house" in the Old Testament is often used to refer to the members of a household or to the family line (See Gen. 7:1, Gen. 28:2, Josh. 24:15, and Prov. 15:27 for examples). God is calling us to build up a Christian heritage — a house that will be faithful to God for many generations into the future.

> *We will not hide them from their children, showing to the generation to come the praises of the LORD, and his strength, and his wonderful works that he hath done. For he established a testimony in Jacob, and appointed a law in Israel, which he commanded our fathers, that they should make them known to their children: That the generation to come might know them, even the children which should be born; who should arise and declare them to their children: That they might set their hope in God, and not forget the works of God, but keep his commandments. (Ps. 78:4-7)*

> *But the mercy of the LORD is from everlasting to everlasting upon them that fear him, and his righteousness unto children's children; To such as keep his covenant, and to those that remember his commandments to do them. (Ps. 103:17 -18)*

Young man, what harvest do you want to reap? Where do you want to be 10 years from now? How about 40 years from now? Growing up and preparing for your future career, marriage and family will not just happen to you! You may have godly parents who will help you and guide you, but to raise and lead your own godly family, you need to form a vision, commit to it, and *work hard.* These precious years of your youth must be invested wisely!

Laziness, both of mind and body, is a great temptation that we young men must overcome by God's help. As we work hard to prepare for our future, our marriages, and our future families, we must rely on God to strengthen us for this task. We cannot complete such a great undertaking in our own strength! As you pursue God's will for your life and your future, remember that God will guide you and give you the strength you need for each new task and responsibility. Pray continually for God's strength and guidance along the way. I pray this book will help you see God's guidance, through His Word and through the guidance of your parents!

> *Trust in the LORD with all your heart, and do not lean on your own understanding. In all your ways acknowledge him, and he will make straight your paths. (Prov. 3:5-6, ESV)*
>
> *But seek first the kingdom of God and his righteousness, and all these things will be added to you. (Matt. 6:33, ESV)*
>
> *I can do all things through Christ which strengtheneth me. (Phil. 4:13)*

A Word to Parents

Parents — your sons need your help! God didn't give young people parents just to care for them and educate them for their first few years. As your children reach adulthood, they will continue to need your advice and guidance, especially as they pursue marriage. Do you remember what you felt like as a young man or woman, anticipating and then launching into the whole new world of marriage and the responsibilities of raising a family? God, in His wisdom, has so timed your life so that you can share your experience and give aid and encouragement to your children when they reach this same stage in their lives. This is part of your responsibility! The next generation of Christian families will render much greater service to King Jesus if it is built on the foundation of earlier generations and their mature faith. Don't make your children and grandchildren start from scratch!

How can you help your sons prepare for marriage? One of the best things you can do is to commit to spending lots of time with your sons. Make it a priority to work on projects together, to take them out for an evening, or to take whatever other opportunities you can to be together and have time to talk. Pursue a growing relationship with your sons during this time in their lives. As sons reach manhood, you should be continually discussing things like vocation, marriage, courtship, and family leadership with them. With frequent times for open discussions, you will be able to teach them much of what they need to know to become godly adults, and they will be comfortable asking questions and bringing up their concerns as well. Spending time together may be harder if your sons are going to school, if they're finished with homeschooling, or if they're already started on college or other training or work that separates you. Even if this is the case, you can still call them, write to them, and make the most of whatever time you do have together.

If this sounds hard, I hope this book will help you! I've tried to arrange these important topics in a format that you and your sons can easily study together. In fact, your sons will learn a lot more from this book (and from you) if you go through the book together. Take time together to discuss the questions, read books and talk about them, and work on some of the projects. Resist temptations to laziness or to letting your children do things the easy way. Study what the Bible says about marriage preparation, and help your sons do it God's way.

What is Covered in this Book?

In this book, we will examine many aspects of Christian marriage preparation. Chapter one begins with our first duty as

Christians, that of putting God first and seeking His glory in all that we do. One of the ways we should put God first in our lives is to regularly attend worship and be a faithful member of Christ's body, the Church. It is also important to firmly understand your doctrinal beliefs so you will know what issues are important, so you can lead and teach your family well, and so you can better evaluate who you (or your children) will be compatible with as a spouse. The Bible tells us not to be unequally yoked with unbelievers.

Although there are many, many aspects of Christian character, we will consider several vital character qualities for a godly man starting a new household. These include accepting responsibility, taking initiative, making wise decisions, and other traits of a godly leader.

Vocational preparation is another essential part of a young man's preparation, and the vocation chapter should help you or your sons evaluate their current vocational standing and map out a strong vocational direction.

Since financial problems are so often at the root of problems in a marriage, I have included several sections on the wise use of money before and after marriage. I also include a short section on the Biblical custom of the bride-price and dowry, a practice that has been nearly forgotten, but one that we would do well to revive.

I have included a chapter on Christian courtship. Several more qualified Christian writers have already written great books on this topic, so I have referred you to these books and not covered the subject in great detail. Still, every courtship will be different, so I hope you will find this chapter helpful!

Perhaps most importantly, a young man must have a godly vision for his *family* before marriage. The final chapter explores the most foundational aspects of a godly family, including marriage, family worship, child training, Christian education, and building a godly heritage.

The Purpose of Prepare Thy Work

This book was written with the following goals in view:

- To help young men to rightly order their actions in this season of life: preparation of callings first, and only afterwards, courtship and marriage.

- To provide help and ideas for parents who desire to help their sons better prepare for marriage. This book is best used as a father/son study.

- To help churches encourage their young men in godly preparation for marriage. The material in this book could easily give structure to a father/son Sunday school class or for a group discussion time with fathers & sons together.

- To help young men study and consider Biblical teaching that applies to marriage preparation.

- To summarize the important aspects of marriage preparation.

- To help young men who are pursuing marriage discern if they are truly ready for marriage.

- To help young men to better feel the gravity of marriage, fatherhood, and family leadership.

- To encourage young men to set goals and approach their future more deliberately.

- To encourage young men to have a strong vision for raising godly families.

- To encourage and direct young men to seek out the counsel of older, wiser, more experienced and godly adults, especially their parents.

- To provide some direction to young men who may not have the blessing of a godly father or other mentor to guide them as they prepare for marriage.

- To provide young men with a few bits of wisdom related to these important topics, and also to direct them to more wisdom found in other books and resources.

- To provide help for parents who desire to evaluate possible future husbands for their daughters.

Reader, it is my prayer that God may use this book to accomplish these purposes in your life, for His glory.

How to Use This Book

This book will be most effective as a father/son study. I have written this book hoping it will be a helpful tool for parents who desire to better prepare their sons for Christian marriage. Young men who aren't able to go through this book with their fathers would do well to find another godly adult or young man to study and discuss questions with. It might work well to meet once a month with another father and son as they go through the book at the same time. Find someone you can be accountable to for the completion of each section. Plan to get together on a regular basis to discuss the questions and your thoughts on each topic. The studies, discussions, and recommended reading will take quite a while to complete, so plan to work through this book over several months or maybe even a year or two. Many of the sections can easily take longer than a month to complete, but the time and effort will be well-spent!

Each topic in this book contains the following subsections; below are some notes and directions for using each section:

Study Scripture:

These sections contain Scripture references related to the section's topic, along with questions to help you think about what you are reading. There are blanks following each question for writing in your answers. In a group or class setting, you may want to complete this study portion individually, and then discuss your answers when you meet together. A concordance or topical Bible may be used to more completely study out many of the questions given.

Examine Yourself:

The questions under this heading are primarily directed to young men, to help them evaluate their present situation and their thinking on the particular topic. These questions should be used for self-examination, in sparking or guiding discussion times, and for group conversation topics.

Hear Counsel:

Most of these points of wisdom are also directed to young men, but many points speak to parents as well. This advice all comes from godly men, teachers, writers, and friends in my own life. During the first stages of writing this book, I interviewed many fathers and recently married men in my church, and this counsel is primarily the result of those interviews. Like the Proverbs, many of these points need not be seen as hard and fast rules, but as the voice of experience, often coming from several different angles. These points of advice will make great fuel for discussion times between sons and parents, with a class group, or with other godly men. This life experience is something we young men lack, and yet desperately need!

Take Action:

All the study, examination, and counsel will be of no use if you don't act on your knowledge! Under this heading, you will find suggested projects to help you grow in each area. Many good books are suggested for your study and growth, some with study questions given in Appendix B of this book. In a group setting, you may choose to do a few projects together as a group and/or give other projects as "homework" assignments. The most important actions are listed under this heading, and additional projects follow under the heading:

For Further Study:

While the assignments under this heading are more optional than those in the **Take Action** section, these additional studies and projects will still be helpful if you have time to do them.

Resources:

The resource lists at the end of each chapter give suggestions of other books, audio recordings, and websites that you may find helpful. I recommend many of these resources in the "Take Action" and "For Further Study" sections, but I have listed some additional resources as well. Appendix A contains a numbered list of suppliers, where most of these resources may be purchased. Numbers in italics *(1, 3, 6)* with each resource listing denote which suppliers each book may be purchased from. Study questions for several of these books are included in Appendix B.

Notes & Goals:

Use this space after each chapter to set your own specific goals, to note your thoughts or convictions, to record additional advice, and to make notes of additional questions or topics for discussion with your parents, sons, or study group.

CHAPTER 1
FAITH & DOCTRINE

*You shall love the LORD your God with all your heart and
with all your soul and with all your might.*
Deuteronomy 6:5 (ESV)

*Let us hear the conclusion of the whole matter: Fear God,
and keep his commandments: for this is the
whole duty of man.*
Ecclesiastes 12:13

*But continue thou in the things which thou hast learned
and hast been assured of, knowing of whom thou hast
learned them;*
*And that from a child thou hast known the holy Scriptures,
which are able to make thee wise unto salvation through
faith which is in Christ Jesus.*
*All Scripture is given by inspiration of God, and is profit-
able for doctrine, for reproof, for correction, for instruction
in righteousness:*
*That the man of God may be perfect, thoroughly furnished
unto all good works.*
2 Timothy 3:14-17

The focus of this chapter is our foundational calling as Christians. As Christian men, each of us should be growing in faith and in love for God throughout our lives, and our desire to serve and glorify God should form the solid foundation for all our other ambitions. Later chapters in this book will discuss our additional callings as workers, husbands, and family leaders, but all these callings must be subject to our life purpose: to bring glory to God in all that we do.

One of the important ways of serving God and remaining faithful is to be a consistent member in a local church body. Furthermore, it is important to have a good grasp of Christian doctrine, founded in God's Word, and to understand your beliefs. As family leaders, we must be articulate about our faith in order to pass this faith to our children.

Put God First

Study Scripture:

1. What are God's most important commandments?

Deut. 6:4-5; Mark 12:29-31

_____

_____

2. How are we to worship God?

1 Sam. 15:22; Ps. 95:6; Matt. 7:21; John 4:24, 14:23; Rom. 12:1

_____

_____

_____

_____

3. Why should we worship God, and Jesus particularly?

Deut. 6:13-15, 10:12-15; Ps. 22:27-28, 29:2a, 86:1-13; Ps. 95-100; Ps. 136:1; Isa. 45:22-23; Matt. 4:10; John 3:16; Rom. 5:6-8, 8:35-39; Eph. 2:4-5; Phil. 2:5-11; Heb. 12:28-29; Rev. 15:4

_____

_____

_____

_____

4. What does God promise to those who love and fear Him?

Deut. 5:29, 7:9; Prov. 3:5-6, 9:10-11, 14:26, 29:25; John 15:4-10; Rom. 8:28

_____

_____

_____

_____

5. What does God say we should be most proud of?

Ps. 34:2, 44:8; Jer. 9:23-24; 2 Cor. 10:17; Gal. 6:14

_____

_____

6. In the following verses, what things are mentioned that men worshipped (or were tempted to worship) instead of God?

Gen. 22:1-14; 1 Sam. 2:27-30; Ps. 115:4; Matt. 6:19-33; Rom. 1:24-25; Gal. 1:10; Col. 3:1-10; 2 Tim. 3:4; 1 John 2:15-17

_____

_____

_____

_____

_____

7. Are you tempted to idolize any of these things? In what ways?

_____

_____

_____

_____

_____

Examine Yourself:

1. Can you think of specific things in your life that drive you or guide your actions more than your desire to serve and please God?

2. What do you think it means to worship God?

3. Why should we worship God?

4. Do you take time every day to read God's Word?

5. Do you take time to pray to God every day? What do you thank Him for? What do you ask Him for?

Hear Counsel:

- Your relationship with God is the foundation for the rest of your life, and for all your other relationships.

- God has given us His Word so that we can truly know Him.

- You can't truly love anyone unless you love God more.

- Be sure you are worshiping God and not idolizing other good things, like success or a good marriage.

- Man is created to worship. Much frustration and confusion comes when we are worshiping (centering our life on) something or someone besides God.

Take Action:

1. Read chapter 2, "A Husband's Understanding of God," and chapter 7, "A Husband's Responsibility: Worshiping Christ Only," in **The Exemplary Husband**, by Stuart Scott.

2. Commit to a consistent time each day for Bible reading and prayer.

3. Pray that God will help you delight in Him and that He will help you be thankful for the way He works in your life.

4. List some ways God has demonstrated His love for you in your life.

For Further Study:

1. Make and follow a plan for memorizing at least one Bible verse each week.

2. Ask your parents or your pastor what it means to "worship."

3. For more projects, Bible studies, and training ideas for young men and parents, see the nine chapters under "Godliness" in **Plants Grown Up**, by Pam Forster.

Embrace Your Christian Calling

Study Scripture:

1. What purposes did God have for man when He created him?

Gen. 1:26-28, 1:31, 2:15

_____

_____

2. What duty did Jesus give His disciples? Does this apply to us as well?

Matt. 28:18-20; Acts 1:8

_____

_____

3. What does Jesus say we should put first? How can you do this?

Matt. 6:33; John 6:27-29

_____

_____

4. Will Christ's kingdom be victorious in history?

Gen. 3:15; Ps. 110:1, 145:13; Isa. 9:6-7, Dan. 2:27-45, 4:34, 6:25-27, 7:9-14; Matt. 6:13; Luke 1:30-33, 13:18-21; 1 Cor. 15:22-28; Heb. 1:8, 12:28

_____

_____

5. What is man's duty?

Deut. 10:12-13; Eccl. 12:13

6. What general principle should we follow in everything we do?

1 Cor. 10:31; Col. 3:23-24

Examine Yourself:

1. Do you feel like you have a strong sense of life purpose? What would you say your life purpose is?

2. Think about different people you know. Who do you think has a strong sense of purpose? Who seems to live without a strong purpose? How can you tell? Have you observed anyone living with an obviously sinful life purpose? Have you observed anyone allowing other non-sinful interests or goals to distract him from more important responsibilities?

3. What unique skills or abilities has God given you? How can you use these to serve others?

4. Are there any particular purposes or goals that God has given you a heart for that you would like to pursue?

5. What specific callings, obligations, or responsibilities do you have right now? Are you fulfilling them well?

6. Young men: which of your callings could a wife help you fulfill better? In what ways could she help you?

7. Married men: in what ways do your wives help you fulfill your callings?

8. Husbands & fathers: what additional callings did you assume when you were married? Young men: are you prepared to assume these additional responsibilities?

Hear Counsel:

- Identify your God-given priorities, and then schedule your time to serve those goals first.

- Some callings are imposed on us, but we often choose to assume the responsibilities of other callings.

- Make a distinction between *obligations* (responsibilities or callings) and *opportunities* (optional things), and be sure your important obligations are being fulfilled before you spend time on opportunities.

- Young men must understand their life purpose before entering marriage. The husband is to be the leader, but he cannot lead if he doesn't know where he is going.

- A young man is ready for a wife only when he is going somewhere and needs help. Just like Adam, you need to tend your own "garden" faithfully. When you need a helper, God will give you one.

- As a young man, it is important to see that whatever position God has placed you in right now, *that is your calling.* You might be a son, a brother, a student, and an employee at this point in your life – these are all callings from God, and faithfulness in these callings is the best preparation for faithfulness in future callings throughout your life.

Take Action:

1. Read **God at Work**, by Gene Edward Veith. Veith draws on Martin Luther's teaching on vocation to help you understand your various callings in life and how God accomplishes His work through his people here on earth. This is foundational material for helping young men understand the significance of their various callings in life. For a more in-depth study of this book, answer the study questions I have given in Appendix B (see pages 184-187).

2. Memorize the answer to the first question in the Westminster Shorter Catechism:

   Q: What is the chief end of man?
   A: Man's chief end is to glorify God and to enjoy Him for ever.

3. Ask your parents what their life purpose is. Ask your friends and older men in your church what they see as their life purpose. Ask them what they see as their most important callings.

4. Pray that you will rightly understand your life purpose, and that God will help you recognize and embrace your specific callings as a Christian.

5. Make a list of the specific callings you have at present in relation to God, your family, your church, and your community and country.

6. We don't choose all our callings, but we do voluntarily assume some of life's very important callings. Consider each of the following contracts and covenants. What do you promise to do in each agreement?

   a. Your baptism
   b. Church membership
   c. A contract for education or a job
   d. Marriage vows
   e. Baptism/dedication of your own children

For Further Study:

1. Read **The Purpose Driven Life**, by Rick Warren.

2. Record your daily activities in detail for one week and evaluate how you are spending your time. What things take up most of your time? Are you being faithful to your present callings? How is God glorified by these daily activities?

3. Listen to **Basement Tapes #2-#5** on the topics of Simple, Separate, and Deliberate living for God's Kingdom. Take a sheet of notebook paper and summarize how you can live out each of these principles as a Christian.

Be Part of the Church Body

Study Scripture:

1. What is Jesus' relationship to the Church?

Eph. 1:22-23, 5:23; Col. 1:18

_____

_____

2. What is the mission of the church?

Matt. 5:14-16, 16:18-19, 28:19-20; 2 Cor. 10:3-6; Rom. 16:20; Eph. 3:21; Rev. 5:9-10

_____

_____

_____

_____

3. How should we observe the Lord's Day? What does the Bible say we should do on this day?

Ex. 20:8, 31:12-17; Lev. 23:3; Isa. 58:13-14; Matt. 12:11-12; Mark 1:21, 2:27-28; Luke 4:31; Acts 13:44, 17:2; Heb. 4:9-11

_____

_____

_____

_____

_____

4. Does the Bible command Christians to meet together?

Heb. 10:24-25

---

5. What should Christians do when assembled together?

Josh. 8:35; Ps. 35:18, 107:32, 111:1, 122:1, 149:1; Acts 2:42; 1 Cor. 14:26, 14:33, 14:40; Col. 3:12-17; Heb. 10:24-25, 1 John 3:16-18

---

6. How should we treat church officers?

Deut. 12:19; 1 Thess. 5:12-13; 1 Tim. 5:17-19; Heb. 13:7, 13:17-18

---

7. What are the Biblical qualifications for an elder?

1 Tim. 3:1-7; Tit. 1:7-9; 1 Pet. 5:1-4

---

8. What are the Biblical qualifications for a deacon?

1 Tim. 3:8-13

_____

_____

_____

_____

9. Read I Cor. 12:1-31. What specific gifts do other members of your church have? (Name at least four different people.)

_____

_____

_____

_____

10. How are they using these gifts to serve?

_____

_____

_____

_____

11. What particular gift or gifts do you believe you have as a member of the Church body?

_____

_____

_____

12. How can you use this gift to serve others in the body?

_____

_____

_____

Examine Yourself:

1. Are you an active member in a Bible-believing, trinitarian church?

2. Are you in submission to your church leadership?

3. If you are not part of a church, what is the reason?

4. Are you confused by any of your church's teachings?

5. Do you disagree with any teachings? How have you or your church officers dealt with these disagreements? Have you made appeals or asked for explanations from the leadership? Have you humbly studied out the issue, or read any material that they recommended?

6. How are you actively serving in your church community?

7. Why is it important to be part of a local church?

Hear Counsel:

- A young man should be in consistent attendance and good standing in a godly Christian church, and be in submission to its authority.

- Being part of a church body will help you grow and give you more opportunities to serve others.

- True maturity is developed under the teaching of God's word and in the community of the church body, not in isolation.

- Churches must believe the Scriptural doctrine of the Trinity — God as Father, Son, and Holy Spirit, Three in One.

Take Action:

1. If you are not a member of a Bible-believing, trinitarian church, find one in your area and attend every week. (Or consider moving near a better church, if there are none nearby.)

2. If you are not already, ask your church elders or deacons for a way you can help serve in your church. (Some examples are setup/cleanup, yard work, repairs, cleaning, music, Sunday school classes, other ministries, etc.)

3. Pray at least once a week for your church leadership.

4. Attend men's meetings at your church.

5. Review and discuss each week's sermon with your family. Take notes and apply the sermon during the week.

For Further Study:

1. Read **A Glorious Church**, by Robert Andrews. Write down or discuss with others his questions after each chapter, and summarize the author's four basic characteristics of a biblical church, found in the conclusion.

2. Read **The Kingdom and the Power**, by Peter Leithart. This book is a thoroughly biblical study of the meaning of the Kingdom of God and the purpose of the church.

3. Read and summarize each point of chapter I, "Of the Worship of God in General," in part III of **A Christian Directory**, by Richard Baxter.

4. Read and summarize each point of chapter XVIII, "Directions for the Holy Spending of the Lord's Day in Families," in part II of **A Christian Directory**, by Richard Baxter.

5. Read and summarize each point of chapter XIX, "Directions for profitable hearing God's word preached," in part II of **A Christian Directory**, by Richard Baxter.

6. For more projects and studies related to this topic, see "Faithfulness in the Church Body" in **Plants Grown Up**, by Pam Forster.

Know What You Believe

Study Scripture:

1. Where should our doctrine come from?

Ps. 1:1-2; 2 Tim. 2:15, 3:14-17; Tit. 1:9

_____

_____

2. What is even more important than hearing God's word?

Matt. 7:24-27; James 2:14-26

_____

3. Does this mean our understanding of God's Word directly affects our actions?

_____

4. Why should leaders and heads of households know God's Word especially well?

Deut. 4:9, 6:6-9; Tit. 1:7-9, 2:1

_____

_____

Examine Yourself:

1. If your parents are faithful believers, have they taught you what they believe?

2. Do you understand it and believe it yourself?

3. Are you ready to teach these truths to your own children?

4. Does your church have a doctrinal statement? Do you understand it and agree with it?

5. Can you explain the gospel to an unbeliever? How often do you take advantages of opportunities to do so?

6. Do you know how to study the Bible? Can you conduct a topical study? Do you know how to study an individual verse, passage, or book of the Bible?

Hear Counsel:

- Memorize Scripture now, and continue to review what you have memorized — the younger you are, the easier it is!

- Your doctrine (what you believe about God and man) will inevitably be played out in the way you live. Base this doctrine on God's Word!

- You need to identify what is important to you, and where you stand on doctrinal issues. Major differences in beliefs will not mix well in a marriage or family, and you will want to discuss some of these possible differences before you commit to marriage.

- Understand spiritual fundamentals so that you can lead your family well, and so that you do not become "unequally yoked" with a wife who has different convictions.

- Be articulate about what you believe, and be ready to teach it to your children.

- Christians should be able to affirm the content of the historic creeds, such as the Apostle's Creed and the Nicene Creed, although it is not necessary for everyone to understand each point entirely.

- Guard against the temptation to be proud or contentious with your doctrinal knowledge — Satan often uses such controversies to divide the church body and put Christians at odds with each other.

Take Action:

1. Read **Essential Truths of the Christian Faith**, by R.C. Sproul. Dr. Sproul's book will give you a basic understanding of doctrinal points that are important for you to understand. If you read one of the short lessons with your Bible reading each day, you can read through all 101 lessons in about 3 months.

2. Pray for understanding as you study different doctrinal issues. Pray that God will teach you through his Word and through the teaching that you receive from others. Pray that you will be prepared to lead your wife and raise your children to know sound doctrine.

3. Learn different methods of Bible study, and schedule times for study. Try to plan at least 30 minutes to an hour at a time, even if it is only one or two times a week.

4. Ask your pastor or church leaders for your churches' doctrinal statement, if they have one. If there is not one, ask your church leadership to explain or write down their basic beliefs. Discuss this with your parents. Do you understand these beliefs?

5. Write at least a paragraph (or a longer paper) on each of these topics, summarizing what you believe about each (be sure to include Scripture references to support your views):

   a) The Bible
   b) God's Sovereignty
   c) Original Sin
   d) Salvation
   e) Baptism and the Lord's Supper
   f) Prayer
   g) The End Times
   h) Ethics
   i) Worship
   j) The Family
   k) The Church

6. After writing your papers, discuss them with your parents,

men from your church, or your pastor. Ask them any questions that you have after thinking through these topics.

For Further Study:

1. Whether with your family, with a group, or on your own, work through **The Westminster Shorter Catechism for Study Classes**, by G. I. Williamson. The Westminster Catechism is a very Scripture-based summary of Christian doctrine, and Williamson's study brings out the full meaning of the catechism and explains many of the biblical truths and proof texts behind each question.

2. Read other historic doctrinal statements of the church, such as the Apostle's Creed, the Nicene Creed, the Council of Chalcedon, and the Athanasian Creed. Talk these over with your parents or your pastor. (See the resources at the end of this chapter for an internet source for these creeds.)

3. Read one or more doctrinal books recommended by your parents or by your pastor, or choose a book from this chapter's resource listing, to study one of the topics you would like to understand better.

Faith & Doctrine Resources:

Essential Truths of the Christian Faith, by R.C. Sproul, published by Tyndale House. *(3, 6)*
A practical, easily understandable summary of Christian doctrine in 102 lessons.

God at Work: Your Christian Vocation in All of Life, by Gene Edward Veith, published by Crossway Books. *(3, 6)*
A very good study of the biblical meaning of vocation, based on Martin Luther's teaching on vocation. Veith explains how God works *through us*, as His instruments, and we don't just work *for Him*. God also ministers to us *through* the actions of other believers around us. This book is highly recommended to everyone! (I've provided study questions for you in Appendix B.)

Don't Waste Your Life, by John Piper, published by Crossway Books. *(3, 6, also available online at www.desiringgod.org)*
Encouragement to help you live your life for the service and glory of God.

Desiring God, by John Piper, published by Multnomah Publishers. *(3, 6 and online at www.desiringgod.org)*
In this book, John Piper shows us that we glorify God best by enjoying Him. Delight in God is our Scriptural duty!

The Purpose Driven Life, by Rick Warren, published by Zondervan. *(3)*
Another helpful study on Christian life purpose.

Easy Chairs, Hard Words, by Douglas Wilson, published by Canon Press. *(2, 3, 6)*
Conversations on God's sovereignty and our salvation.

Tearing Down Strongholds, by R.C. Sproul, Jr., published by P&R Publishing. *(3, 6, 8)*

Tools for defending Christianity and tearing down other prevalent, yet false worldviews.

The Westminster Standards, published by Great Commission Publications. *(5)*
Includes the Westminster Confession of Faith, the Larger Catechism, and the Shorter Catechism. All these documents were written by church leaders in the 17th century to summarize and aid in teaching biblical doctrine. These historic works are so Bible-based that they still give an excellent summary of Christian doctrine for us to study.

The Westminster Shorter Catechism for Study Classes, by G. I. Williamson, published by P & R Publishing. *(1, 3, 5)*
This study guide for the Westminster Shorter Catechism gives a clear explanation of each of the catechism's questions, along with Scripture proofs. Excellent for an individual or group study on Christian doctrine.

A Christian Directory, by Richard Baxter, published by Soli Deo Gloria Publications. *(7)*
Volume one of **The Practical Works of Richard Baxter**, a Puritan author. This book is packed with practical, biblical directions for Christian living, including personal holiness, family duties, and matters of church and state. Nearly all of these directions are just as applicable today as they were when they were written. This is an amazing resource!

Mere Christianity, by C. S. Lewis, published by Zondervan. *(3, 6)*
A plain explanation of Christianity and Christian living without a particular denominational bias.

A Glorious Church, by Robert Andrews, published by Sentinel Press. *(Available from Amazon.com)*
Bible-based guidelines for the mission, structure, and ministry of the church.

The Kingdom and the Power, by Peter Leithart, published by
P&R Publishing. *(3)*
Examines the Bible's teaching on the purpose of the
church and the meaning of the "Kingdom of God."

God's Law in the Modern World, by Kenneth Gentry,
published by the Institute for Christian Economics.
(Available from Amazon.com)
A concise argument for the proper use of the Old Testament Law.

Unconditional Surrender, by Gary North, published by the
Institute for Christian Economics. *(6)*
A study of Biblical implications for man, the church, civil
government, and our view of the future.

**Basement Tapes #2-#5, Conversations on Living Life Sim-
ply, Living Life Separately, Living Life Deliberately,
and Building the Kingdom**, produced and distributed
by the Highlands Study Center. *(8)*
Available individually or as **The HSC Motto** set, these
are recorded conversations on topics foundational to our
Christian life purpose.

Center for Reformed Theology and Apologetics.
http://www.reformed.org/documents
An excellent internet source for historic Christian creeds
and confessions.

Faith & Doctrine Notes:

_____

_____

_____

_____

_____

_____

_____

_____

_____

_____

_____

_____

_____

_____

_____

_____

_____

_____

_____

_____

Faith & Doctrine Goals:

_____

_____

_____

_____

_____

_____

_____

_____

_____

_____

_____

_____

_____

_____

_____

_____

_____

_____

_____

_____

CHAPTER 2

GODLY MANHOOD

Wherewithal shall a young man cleanse his way? by
taking heed thereto according to thy word.
Psalm 119:9

When first planning this book, I had originally planned a larger section on Christian character, but with so many different Christian character qualities to consider, this chapter quickly began to take over the whole book! Consequently, the character qualities discussed in this chapter are those I considered the *most* pertinent to young men preparing for marriage and family leadership.

For a more complete study of Christian character for young men, see another book from Doorposts, **Plants Grown Up**. This book, written by my mother, covers over 50 godly character qualities, giving Bible studies, projects, and evaluation questions for each topic. Parents will find this book to be a valuable tool for training both younger and older sons.

Accept Responsibility

Study Scripture:

1. What happens to the man who is faithful with what he is given?

Gen. 39:1-6, 39:21-23, 41:38-41; 1 Sam. 18:5; Luke 12:42-44, 16:10-12, 19:12-26

_____

_____

_____

2. What comes with greater positions and greater blessings?

Luke 12:48; Rom. 15:1; James 3:1

_____

_____

3. What effect does a faithful man have on others?

Prov. 25:13

_____

_____

4. What kind of person makes excuses?

Prov. 26:13

_____

_____

5. What happens to men who make excuses?

Num. 13:30-33, 14:20-24; 1 Sam. 13:11-14, 15:13-28; Prov. 20:4

_____

_____

_____

_____

Examine Yourself:

1. Do you faithfully carry out the tasks that parents, teachers, and employers give you?

2. Do they usually need to check up on your work and correct your mistakes?

3. Do you make excuses when you are corrected?

4. Do you follow through when you have given your word that you will do something?

5. Have you ever been given greater responsibility after handling a smaller task well?

6. What are some of the responsibilities you have right now?

7. Do you think you are ready to assume the responsibilities of a husband and father?

Hear Counsel:

- Responsibility is not something you can take or leave! A man will either take responsibility well, or he will take it poorly, but he cannot get away from responsibility that he has been given.

- To successfully lead in any area of life, you must learn to accept responsibility for your own actions and even for the actions of those under your care. A young man must understand the gravity of responsibility before pursuing marriage, because he will be ultimately responsible for himself, his wife, and his children.

- Young men must learn to fulfill their responsibilities whole-heartedly, and, when they fail, not to make excuses.

- Employers will value and promote a man who takes his responsibilities seriously.

- Greater responsibility often comes to men who are faithful in smaller responsibilities.

- As with most character qualities, responsibility is easier to learn early in life, in the small tasks you are given at home. If your parents have helped you learn to take responsibility, thank them! If they are still training you, listen to them and start learning now!

- Although living all by yourself is usually not wise, moving out of your parents' home and living on your own at some point can force you to take more responsibility.

- When you are married, be prepared to delegate responsibilities to your wife. Let her make decisions, especially in her domain of homemaking.

Take Action:

1. For an excellent summary of the responsibilities of a husband and father, read **Mighty Men: The Starter's Guide to Leading Your Family**, by John Crotts. Summarize each of the four sections and discuss the book with your parents.

2. Read chapter 8, "Leadership — a Certain Sound," in **The Family, God's Weapon for Victory**, by Robert Andrews.

3. Read chapter 2, "Effeminacy and Biblical Masculinity," in **Future Men**, by Douglas Wilson.

4. Pray that you would see and repent of any excuse-making, and of any failures to fulfill your own responsibilities.

5. Make a list of your present responsibilities in your home, church, and workplace. Are you fulfilling these responsibilities faithfully? When was the last time you volunteered to take on a new responsibility?

6. Choose one area of responsibility that you need to improve in. Pray about it and work to better fulfill your responsibility.

7. Make a list of responsibilities you will have as a husband. Make a list of additional responsibilities you will have as a father. For each area of future responsibility, list at least one way you can be actively preparing for this responsibility now.

For Further Study:

1. Read chapters 1-7 in **Family Man, Family Leader**, by Philip Lancaster.

2. After reading Chapter 3, "The Man Is Responsible," in **Family Man, Family Leader**, answer these questions:

   A. What 7 reasons does he find in Genesis 2-3 that inform our understanding of the husband's headship?

   B. What 5 qualities did Adam lack that contributed to man's fall?

   C. What are the 3 important truths you should remember from this chapter?

3. Read the following Bible accounts of men in authority who made excuses for their mistakes: *Gen. 3:9-19, Ex. 32:1-24, and 1 Sam. 15:1-23.*

   Was God pleased with them? Were others pleased with them? What happened to them?

4. Make and implement a plan to help you stop making excuses. Ask your family and friends to help you.

Serve Others

Study Scripture:

1. According to Jesus, what do great men do? What examples has Jesus set for us here?

Matt. 20:25-28, 23:11-12; Luke 22:26; John 13:14-15; Rom. 15:1-3; Phil. 2:3-8

_____

_____

_____

_____

2. How are we to serve one another?

Gal. 5:13; Eph. 6:7; Col. 3:12-14

_____

_____

3. As a husband and father, who will you be set over and also most obligated to serve?

Eph. 5:23; 1 Tim. 5:8

_____

4. Who else should we serve?

Gal. 6:10

_____

_____

Examine Yourself:

1. Do you look for ways to serve your family and friends, or do you want them to serve you all the time?

2. Are you thankful for those who serve you? How do you demonstrate this thankfulness?

3. Do you resent doing "more than your share"?

4. Do you serve others humbly and sincerely, or do you serve out of a desire to impress or manipulate others?

Hear Counsel:

- A large part of godly leadership is serving those under your care — follow the example that Jesus set for us as leaders.

- When you are young, it's easy to think that being in authority just means being in charge. When you become a husband and father yourself, you will find that your parents were serving you a lot more than you thought!

Take Action:

1. Read chapter 5, "Manhood Under the Cross," in **Family Man, Family Leader**, by Philip Lancaster.

2. Watch your parents for a day and write down each thing they do to serve others.

3. Look for ways you can serve your own family. Offer to help your parents with some of their duties so that they have some free time. Think of things you can do for your brothers and sisters to please them.

4. Commit to serving your grandparents, if this is possible and if you are not already doing it consistently. What kind of work can you do for them to bless them? What needs do they have?

5. Ask the deacons in your church if there is any job you can do to serve the church.

6. Go out of your way to thank those who are in authority over you for serving you.

7. Read through the book of Mark and write down every thing that Jesus does to serve others.

For Further Study:

1. Find someone in your church who needs help with a project (yard work, moving, remodeling, etc.), and offer them your help.

2. Find a specific avenue of service in your community. Think of political service, service at rest homes/senior centers, and service for younger families, neighbors, or widows.

3. For more projects that will help you learn to be a servant, see the chapters on "Serving Others with a Cheerful Heart" and "Giving Up Our Own Desires," in **Plants Grown Up**, by Pam Forster.

Take Initiative

Study Scripture:

1. Who tells the ants when to work?

Prov. 6:6-8

_____

_____

2. What happens to the man who doesn't act on his own initiative?

Prov. 12:24, 21:25

_____

_____

_____

3. What are we doing if we fail to do what we know is right?

James 4:17

_____

Examine Yourself:

1. Are you usually aware of problems, tasks needing to be done, or opportunities to serve?

2. Do you avoid, complain about, and make excuses about these things, or do you take appropriate action?

3. Do you wait for others to do a task instead of doing it yourself?

Hear Counsel:

- A young man is not ready to get married if he does not have a habit of exercising initiative.

- Having responsibility requires you to take initiative – many of your responsibilities must be fulfilled without anyone telling you what to do.

- When you are a husband and father, there will be many things that will go wrong or simply won't happen if you don't learn to take initiative. As the leader of your family, you will need to make decisions and act when no one is telling you what to do.

Take Action:

1. Get out of bed on time on your own initiative.

2. At home, while doing school, or while at work, perform as many duties as you can before someone has to tell you to do them or remind you about them.

3. Find several projects or jobs around your home that need to be done, talk with your parents, and offer to do what needs to be done. Then follow through with your commitments.

4. When you see your mother or sisters inconvenienced by a problem, take action to help them if you are able.

5. Practice initiating conversations with others as you have opportunity.

For Further Study:

1. When you are annoyed or inconvenienced by a problem, take action to resolve the problem, rather than waiting for someone else to deal with it.

2. Suggest a family activity and take steps to make it happen.

3. For more projects and Bible studies related to this topic, see "Leadership: Excercising Initiative," in **Plants Grown Up**, by Pam Forster.

Make Wise Decisions

Study Scripture:

1. Where does wisdom come from?

Ps. 32:8, 73:24, 119:66; Prov. 1:7, 2:1-7, 3:5-6, 9:10

_____

_____

_____

2. How can we get it?

1 Kings 3:9; Prov. 2:1-7; James 1:5

_____

_____

3. What else can help us make wise decisions?

1 Kings 12:1-16; Prov. 1:8, 6:20-23, 12:15, 13:10, 13:14, 15:22, 19:20, 20:18

_____

_____

_____

4. Will the Holy Spirit lead us in a direction contrary to the Bible's teaching?

Deut. 4:2; John 14:23-26; John 16:13

_____

Examine Yourself:

1. Do you ask for and listen to counsel from those involved when you are making a decision?

2. What difficult decisions have you faced?

3. Do you see any other difficult decisions facing you in the near future?

4. Do you make your decisions based on Scriptural principles, or do you make them based on your own feelings?

5. Do you pray when making a decision?

Hear Counsel:

▪ Have a plan for making large and small decisions, know how to seek counsel.

▪ Resist the temptation to think that you have it all figured out! A wiser, more experienced person will often have good advice to give if you are willing to listen. Listen to Solomon—"Hear, my son, your father's instruction, and forsake not your mother's teaching!" (Prov. 1:8, ESV)

▪ Making wise decisions in the varying situations of life takes understanding and wisdom, which God says he will give us if we ask. We must pray for wisdom and study God's Word, seeking to apply it to the different decisions we face.

Take Action:

1. Read **Step by Step**, by James Petty, and summarize each step of the decision-making process he describes.

2. When making hard decisions about your schooling, job, career direction, etc., do all you can to make a wise decision: Study Scripture, pray about it, ask for counsel from your parents and men you know.

3. Humbly listen to advice that others give you, even if you didn't ask for it.

For Further Study

1. Make a list of people you could ask for counsel when you are faced with a hard decision.

2. For more projects and Bible studies related to this topic, see "Leadership: Making Godly Decisions," in **Plants Grown Up**, by Pam Forster.

Submit to God-given Authorities

Study Scripture:

1. Why should we honor earthly authorities?

Rom. 13:1-2

---

2. What earthly authorities are we to honor most? How can we do this? What blessings will it bring? What happens to those who disobey this command?

Ex. 20:12; Prov. 1:8-9, 4:1, 4:20-22, 6:20-24, 7:1-5, 13:1, 15:5, 15:10, 15: 20, 17:6, 19:13, 19:26, 23:15-16, 23:22-26, 27:11, 28:7, 28:24, 29:3, 29:15, 29:17, 30:11, 30:17; Eph. 6:1-3

3. How should we relate to civil authorities? What if they are ungodly?

Matt. 23:1-3; Acts 5:29; Rom. 13:1-7; 1 Tim. 2:1-3; 1 Pet. 2:13-21

_____

_____

_____

_____

_____

4. What happened to these people in the Bible who did not honor the authorities God placed over them?

Num. 12, 16; 2 Sam. 15:1-18:17

_____

_____

_____

Examine yourself:

1. Do you give honor and respect to your parents, knowing that God has put you together for good?

2. Do you speak to your parents in a respectful manner?

3. Do you honor your parents by the way you speak about them to others?

4. Do you pray for your parents regularly?

5. Do you thank your parents for the blessing of their authority, love, provision, and protection? Do you thank God for giving you these blessings through your parents?

6. Do you cheerfully and respectfully obey your parents' godly commands and receive their godly counsel?

7. Do you listen to your parents' corrections and repent of sins they bring to your attention?

8. Do you support and build up your parents as the authorities in your home? Are you loyal to them and their leadership?

9. Do you show patience and love to your parents, forgiving them for sins that they commit against you?

10. Do your actions bring honor and joy to your parents? Does your life build up their reputation?

11. Have you been negligent in fulfilling any of the above duties to your parents?

12. Ask yourself these questions again, inserting "church leaders," "teachers," "boss at work," and "civil authorities" in the place of "parents."

13. In what ways do you need to change most in how you view and treat the authorities in your life?

Hear Counsel:

- Respect and submit to authority God has placed you under.

- A good leader must first know how to respect and submit to authority.

- Be teachable and humble. Accept advice from godly people, ESPECIALLY YOUR PARENTS!

- Boys should remain under their father's authority until marriage. Until then, they should be increasing in responsibility to the point that they know their father's heart and no longer need his oversight. After marriage, the son is not under the father's authority, and the father can only give advice. The son, as a husband, is now directly accountable to Jesus Christ. Man was not designed to be out from under authority and without any responsibilities (Robert Andrews in **The Family, God's Weapon for Victory**).

- Submission to the authority over you liberates you to pursue your specific callings and to rule well in your own realms of authority.

- Biblical meekness is not weakness; it is strength in submission to authority.

- Sons are to "leave the home" in a sense. Some do not do this in the right way. Fathers should raise their sons up to have a proper level of independence, while still seeking counsel and honoring their parents.

Take Action:

1. Read Chapter 5, "Honor Your Father and Mother," in **Make It Your Ambition**, by John Notgrass.

2. Use **For This Is Right**, by Pam Forster, as a tool to evaluate your submission to your parents and other authorities in your life. Review the summary questions every week, and study in more detail any areas that you are struggling in.

3. Pray regularly for your parents, your grandparents, your church leaders, your civil rulers, and any other authorities in your life. Make cards, a small notebook, or something else to help you keep track of specific ways you can pray for each of them.

For Further Study:

1. Listen to **The Promise**, a message on the 5th Commandment by Doug Phillips.

2. Learn from the examples of the authorities over you. Which authorities are easiest to follow? Why?

3. For more projects and Bible studies related to this topic, see "Obeying God and His Authorities," in **Plants Grown Up**, by Pam Forster.

Set and Follow Good Examples

Study Scripture:

1. Jesus expects us to follow His example. What examples has He set for us?

Lev. 11:45; Luke 6:36; John 13:13-17, 13:34; Phil. 2:5-8; Col. 3:13; Heb. 12:1-3; 1 Pet. 2:21-23; 1 John 3:16

---

2. Who else should we follow the examples of?

Prov. 23:26; 1 Cor. 11:1; Phil. 3:17, 4:9; Heb. 13:7

---

3. How will the company we keep affect us?

1 Kings 11:1-6; Ps. 1; Prov. 1:10-19, 13:20; 1 Cor. 15:33; Heb. 10:24-25

Examine Yourself:

1. How can you better follow Jesus' example, as seen in the verses above?

2. What kind of example do you set for your siblings and friends? Are you setting a godly example in speech, in conduct, in love, in faith, and in purity (1 Tim. 4:12)?

3. What kind of people do you spend most of your time with? Are they the kind of people you want to be like?

4. What kind of example have your parents set for you?

5. Where they have set a good example, are you following it?

6. If you were a father now, what do you think your children would learn from your example?

7. What other godly men in history do you admire and look up to?

8. What character qualities do they have that you can imitate?

Hear Counsel:

- Be careful of the company you keep. *Who you spend time with shapes who you are,* so spend time with those who you want to be like.

- Cultivate strong, open relationships with your family and other mature men. Spend lots of time with people and learn to get along with them and serve them.

- Spending the majority of your time with your peers is not a good thing. It will not help you grow in godly character.

- If you spend time with those of poor character, you should have a positive effect on them. Otherwise, you should avoid them.

- As a father, your example may be the strongest shaping influence on your children, whether it is for good or ill.

- Fathers, many important character qualities are taught by example! Your life and marriage is the most powerful training tool for your sons.

- God's character is the greatest example for us, and we are told to imitate his holiness.

Take Action:

1. Think of any siblings or friends who look up to you as an example. Consider the example you are setting when you are around them. Which of your traits would you *not* want them to imitate?

2. Make a list of all the people you spend time with during a week. Decide whether each one sets a good example or a bad example for you. Whose examples are you following? Who are you setting a good example for?

3. Think of a way that you can spend more time with godly men who will be a good example to you. Think of ways you can learn from them, work with them, or serve them.

4. Study the lives of other Christians in history who were known for their strong character. Here is a list to get you started:

Athanatius	Robert E. Lee
Augustine	David Livingstone
J. S. Bach	Martin Luther
Dietrich Bonhoeffer	D. L. Moody
William Booth	John Newton
William Bradford	John G. Paton
Martin Bucer	Patrick (known as St. Patrick)
John Calvin	Francis Schaeffer
William Carey	Charles Spurgeon
Jonathan Edwards	Hudson Taylor
Jim Elliot	William Wallace
Stonewall Jackson	George Whitefield
Adoniram Judson	John Wycliffe
John Knox	

For Further Study:

1. Make your own list of godly character qualities. Beside each one, list someone you know (or that you have heard about) who clearly demonstrates this quality. Pick at least two of these character qualities that you feel a need to grow in, and plan a way you can follow the good example of the person you listed.

2. For more projects and Bible studies related to this topic, see the chapters "Leadership: Setting a Godly Example" and "Developing Godly Relationships," in **Plants Grown Up**, by Pam Forster.

Flee from Lust

Study Scripture:

1. What is the full meaning of the 7th commandment?

Ex. 20:14; Job 31:1; Matt. 5:27-28

---

2. What does God say we are to do with our lusts? What is to take the place of these lusts in our hearts?

Rom. 13:14; 1 Cor. 6:18-20; Eph. 5:3-4; Col. 3:5-6; 1 Thess. 4:3-5; 2 Tim. 2:22

---

3. What is the Bible's advice for avoiding lust and sexual sin?

Gen. 39:12; Ps. 101:3; Prov. 2, 5, 6:20-24, 7:1-5; Rom. 12:9; 1 Cor. 7:2; Heb. 13:4

---

4. What is the end result of lust and sexual sins?

Lev. 20:10; Prov. 2:16-19, 5:3-11, 6:27-29, 6:32-33, 7:25-27; Eph. 5:5; Heb. 13:4; James 1:15

_____

_____

_____

_____

Examine Yourself:

1. Do you exercise self-control over your appetites? Or do you have problems controlling how much you eat, sleep, or play?

2. Do you guard your thoughts and eyes, and pray that God will help you fight temptations to lust?

3. Do you avoid and flee situations that bring temptations to lust?

4. Do you rely on God's help to resist lust, or do you try to fight it by your own strength only?

5. Are you committed to preserving your physical and emotional purity, waiting for the wife that God, in His providence, may someday give you?

6. Do you show honor and respect to the girls and women in your life?

Hear Counsel:

- Parents must guide sons from birth. Teach them to control their appetites at an early age, or it probably won't happen. Many of these lessons can only be learned as a young child.

- Teach sons to obey from the start.

- Purity includes your mind and emotions, not just your body.

- General idleness and failure to love those we should be loving makes us more susceptible to temptations to idle and lustful thoughts.

- Be very careful not to stir up emotions (in girls or in yourself) before commitments are made (see more about this in the courtship chapter).

- Protect girls around you from men who are not their husband, including yourself!

- On government of the eyes: "Remember still how much more easy and safe it is, to stop sin here at the gates and outworks, than to beat it out again when it is once got in: if it have but tainted your very fantasy or memory, (as tempting sights will almost unavoidably do,) it hath there spawned the matter for a swarm of vain and sinful thoughts. It is almost impossible to rule the thoughts without ruling the eye..."

  "Keep both eye and mind employed in continual duty, and let them not be idle, and have leisure to wander upon vanity...Let your spiritual work and your lawful bodily labours, take up your time and thoughts, and command and keep your senses in their services."

  "Beg daily of God the preserving assistance of his grace and providence."
  *(From **A Christian Directory,** by Richard Baxter, p.307)*

Take Action:

1. Read **Sex Is Not the Problem (Lust Is)**, by Joshua Harris, (first released as **Not Even a Hint**) and answer the study questions I've provided on page 195.

2. Read chapter 20, "A Husband's Regret: Lust," in **The Exemplary Husband**, by Stuart Scott.

3. Make a specific plan to avoid places and situations that tempt you to lust.

4. Make specific plans to fight lustful thoughts by replacing them with prayer, reviewing memorized Scripture, and loving actions toward others. Pray for God's help as you do this.

5. Write out your commitment to purity of thoughts, eyes, speech, and actions before marriage. Share this with your father or another godly man, and ask him to hold you accountable.

For Further Study:

1. Read **Fidelity**, by Douglas Wilson.

2. Read and summarize Richard Baxter's "Directions against inward, filthy Lusts," (chapter VIII, part V, tit. 2) from **A Christian Directory**. His chapters of directions for governing the passions and governing the eyes also offer practical and pointed advice for growing in purity.

3. For more projects and Bible studies related to this topic, see the chapters "Self-Control over the Thought Life" and "Fleeing Temptation," in **Plants Grown Up**, by Pam Forster.

Godly Manhood Resources

The Disciplined Life, by Richard S. Taylor, published by
Bethany House. *(3)*
Another must-read for all young men! This small, powerful book emphasizes the necessity of self-discipline in
the life of every Christian.

The Family, God's Weapon for Victory, by Robert Andrews,
published by Sentinel Press. *(5, 6)*
A very practical handbook for fathers and husbands, this
book is full of wise advice from Mr. Andrews, all based
on Scripture and his many experiences as a husband,
father, and pastor. Highly recommended!

Family Man, Family Leader, by Philip Lancaster, published by
Vision Forum. *(1, 3, 6, 7,10)*
A thorough Biblical study for a head of a household. This
book will help you better imitate God's character as you
lead your wife and children.

Mighty Men: The Starter's Guide to Leading Your Family, by
John Crotts, published by Grace and Truth Books. *(3, 7)*
An extremely practical, concise outline of a family
leader's God-given duties. Highly recommended!

Step by Step, by James C. Petty, published by P&R Publishing.
(3, 6)
Of the many books on Christian decision making, this is
the best I've read.

Robert E. Lee on Leadership, by H. W. Crocker III, published
by Three Rivers Press. *(Available from Amazon.com)*
Lessons in godly leadership from the life of a godly
Christian man.

Future Men, by Douglas Wilson, published by Canon Press.
(1, 2, 3, 5, 6, 7)
Examines true, biblical masculinity and adresses
common issues with raising boys. (I have provided study
questions for this book in Appendix B.)

Boyood and Beyond, by Bob Schultz, published by Great
Expectations Book Co. *(6)*
Sound advice, based on Scripture and life experience, for
boys who are on the road to becoming men of honor,
courage, and faith.

Created for Work, by Bob Schultz, published by Great Expectations Book Co. *(6)*
Encouragement for young men to develop a God-honor-
ing attitude toward work.

Spiritual Disciplines For the Christian Life, by Donald S.
Whitney, published by NavPress. *(3, 7)*
A helpful study on the importance and methods of spiritual disciplines, including Bible reading, prayer, worship, evangelism, serving others, and more.

The Pursuit of Holiness, by Jerry Bridges, published by
NavPress. *(3)*
God says we are to "be holy, as he is holy." This book
helps believers see the need for holy living and discipline
their lives accordingly.

**What's the Difference? Manhood and Womanhood Defined
According to the Bible**, by John Piper, published by
Crossway Books. *(3, also available online at
www.desiringgod.org)*
An excellent study on the Bible's glorious, yet very differ-
ent roles for men and women.

The Mark of a Man, by Elisabeth Elliot, published by Baker
Book House. *(3, 7)*
Letters to a young man on what authentic manhood
really is.

Sex is Not the Problem, Lust Is (first printed as **Not Even a Hint**), by Joshua Harris, published by Multnomah Publishers. *(3, 6, 7)*
Encouragement, all based on Scripture, to help both young men and women fight temptations to lust. (I have provided study questions for this book in Appendix B.)

Fidelity, by Douglas Wilson, published by Canon Press. *(1, 2, 3, 6, 7)*
A biblical perspective on purity and being a "one woman man."

Plants Grown Up, by Pam Forster, published by Doorposts. *(1, 5, 6, 7)*
Bible studies and projects to help build Christian character in sons.

Biblical Masculinity, audio sermons by Pastor Steve Wilkins, produced by Covenant Media Foundation. *(4)*
A series of 21 sermons exploring biblical masculinity and the particular callings of men.

The Promise, audio message by Doug Phillips, published by Vision Forum. *(3, 6, 10)*
The Fifth Commandment comes with a promise, and Doug Phillips helps us see just how important and glorious it is to obey this commandment.

Godly Manhood Notes:

_____

_____

_____

_____

_____

_____

_____

_____

_____

_____

_____

_____

_____

_____

_____

_____

_____

_____

_____

_____

_____

_____

_____

Godly Manhood Goals:

Chapter 3

Vocation

*The LORD God took the man and put him in the garden of
Eden to work it and keep it.*
Genesis 2:15 (ESV)

Six days you shall labor, and do all your work.
Exodus 20:9 (ESV)

*Prepare thy work without, and make it fit for thyself in the
field; and afterwards build thine house.*
Proverbs 24:27

Although it is not our only focus in marriage preparation, preparing for your career *is* one of the clearest applications of Proverbs 24:27. Young men must use these early years to establish their career direction, learning skills that will serve others and support a family. Young men, if you are going to provide adequately for a wife and children, you need to use your time wisely **right now!** Start identifying your gifts, refining your skills, studying available occupations, and getting advice about your career direction in your early teen years.

Choose Your Career Direction

Study Scripture:

1. Some things can only be done in the right season. Are you taking advantage of this season of your life to prepare yourself for the next?

Prov. 10:5, 20:4, 24:27, 30:24-25; Eccl. 3:1

---

2. What should we have when we are making big decisions like choosing a career direction?

Prov. 11:14, 15:22, 20:18

---

3. Does God give specific gifts or talents to different people?

Ex. 35:30-35; Dan. 1:17; Rom. 12:4-8; 1 Cor. 7:7, 12:4-11; 1 Tim. 4:14; 1 Pet. 4:10-11

---

4. Why should we be well established in a career direction?

Prov. 12:24, 22:29; 1 Thess. 4:9-12; 2 Thess. 3:10-12; 1 Tim. 5:8

---

5. Whatever direction we choose, how should we pursue our work?

Eccl. 9:10a; Col. 3:23-24

_____

_____

_____

Examine Yourself:

1. Do you accept full responsibility for providing for your future family, should God bless you with one?

2. Are you already established in a godly career path?

3. If not, what directions could you go with your present training and skills?

4. What interests or passions do you have?

5. What kind of problems do you like to solve?

6. What kind of work experience do you have right now?

7. What kind of work do you really enjoy doing?

8. Are there any kinds of work that sound enjoyable that you could learn more about?

9. What options do you have for getting vocational training?

10. Have you saved any money to spend on your education?

11. If you are planning to work for someone else, can you work under a godly man in a business run according to godly principles instead of furthering the purposes of an unbeliever?

12. What is your opinion on self-employment?

13. How much experience do you have in self-directed work?

14. Do you have the personality and maturity to rule yourself or

others, or do you work better under the direction of others?

15. Do you finish what you start?

16. Have you saved any money that you could invest in starting a business?

Hear Counsel:

- Young men MUST be established in or at least well on the path to their vocation before they move towards marriage. Their course should be plotted out.

- Young men with vague ideas of vocation (or no ideas at all) are a serious problem today, even in the church.

- Being established in a career path with goals is a lot different than just having a "good job."

- Know what it will cost to support a household, and make plans for earning enough money to consistently pay for necessities. You need to have the costs of living covered by your income, or it will be very hard to keep your wife at home and stay out of debt.

- Career direction is one of the big decisions you have to make as a young man. The earlier you make the choice, the more time you will have to gain experience and move ahead, but since the choice will influence the rest of your life, you must make it wisely and carefully. This decision takes a great deal of wisdom, and the ability to see your personality and gifts honestly—you need to pray, study the Bible, and seek advice from your parents and other godly adults as you make this decision!

- These are some of the most important criteria for a godly career choice:

    1. It must *exercise dominion* over God's creation in some way. *(Gen. 1:28)*
    2. It must allow you to *serve others* in some way. *(Luke 22:26, Gal. 5:13)*

3. It must allow you to *provide an adequate living for you and your family. (1 Tim. 5:8)*

4. It should *give you some sort of enjoyment and satisfaction. (Eccl. 5:18-20)*

5. It should, as much as possible, *match your God-given talents and abilities. (Ex. 31:1-6; Rom. 12:6-8; 1 Pet. 4:10-11)*

- If you are having a hard time making a decision, it is better for you to start working and pursuing a *good* career, rather than waiting around for the *perfect* one to come along. At some point, you just have to pick the best thing you can, work hard, and trust God with the results.

- If you are doing your best to please God in your career choice, he can make it work out for the best even if you don't end up in the same career for your whole life. Working in different fields can prepare you for other types of work you might never even dream of now!

- Don't let yourself be paralyzed by the importance of this decision! You probably won't find a career that seems perfect in every way, and at some point, you will just have to make the best choice you can given your circumstances and forge ahead!

- You will have opportunities to witness for Christ whether you are an employee or a business owner, just in different ways.

- Being responsible is better than being rich.

- Starting out self-employed can be difficult, risky, or even impossible in some situations. It may be prudent for someone with a vision for self-employment to spend many years as an employee, working faithfully for others, before he establishes his own business.

- *Self-employment* takes *self-discipline*!

- Self-employment often involves greater risk. Some employment positions (like sales) also involve risk. Willingness to take risks can allow you to earn more, if you are skilled or experienced at your work.

■ Consider doing what your parents do for work, especially if they are business owners or self-employed. Through much of history, this has worked well, but our culture today has reacted against it. There is no reason that *everyone* must go to college and sample *every possible* career before choosing one! There is a pretty good chance that, out of a larger family, one or two children will have similar character, abilities, and desires as the parents. There are many benefits that come with following your parents: you can learn along side them, your help can be a blessing to them, and, if they are self-employed, you may be able to manage or inherit their established business some day.

Take Action:

1. Read **Your Career in Changing Times**, by Lee Ellis & Larry Burkett.

2. Complete a "personality survey," such as the one included in **Finding the Career That Fits You**, by Larry Burkett, and find out what types of careers match your personality strengths. This particular survey uses the DISC model, and outlines 4 main traits: Dominant, Influencing, Steady, and Conscientious. Find which traits you have high and low levels of, and then look at which careers are normally a good fit for your combination of strengths and weaknesses. (Both **Finding the Career That Fits You** and **Your Career in Changing Times** will help you do this.)

3. Ask your parents, grandparents, or other godly men from your church what strengths or gifts they see in you.

4. Use the "Career Choice Evaluation Sheet" on pages 207-208 to evaluate two or more career possibilities (including the job you have and any other careers that you are seriously interested in).

5. Review the section on "Making Wise Decisions" in Chapter 2.

6. Pray for wisdom in making your career choice.

7. Ask self-employed men you know about the challenges they face. What strengths are required to be self-employed? What are the benefits of being self-employed?

8. Talk to men who work for an employer. Why did they choose to work for this employer? What advantages come with working for someone else?

9. Begin helping your father with his work, if that is possible. Maybe you can go to work with him for a day, or for a week, and get an idea of what he does. There may be other men that you can try this with as well.

10. List some ways that you could share the Gospel as an employee or as a business owner.

For Further Study:

1. Listen to "Getting the Big Picture for Entrepreneurship and the Christian Family," the introductory address from **The Best of the 2006 Entrepreneurial Bootcamp**, produced by Vision Forum.

2. Listen to "The Biblical Basis for Family Business," by Gregg Harris, from the **Home and Family Business Workshop** tape series.

3. Compare regular employment and self-employment, and list the advantages and disadvantages of each. You may want to ask your parents and men from your church to help you. Ask your parents if they think you have the qualities necessary for self-employment.

4. For whatever career direction you choose, make specific plans for spending enough time away from your work and with your family (both present and future).

5. Choose a short-term job or project that you can take charge of and see to completion, to get experience in self-directed work.

6. If you already have a lot of self-directed projects completed or in progress, make a list of them. How many have you finished? Were any left unfinished?

Pursue Your Career Direction

Study Scripture:

1. Does God command us to work?

Ex. 20:9; 2 Thess. 3:10-12

_____

_____

2. What examples do ants set that we should follow?

Prov. 6:6-8; 30:24-25

_____

_____

3. What are the results of laziness?

Prov. 6:9-11, 10:4-5, 13:4, 14:23, 15:19, 18:9, 20:4, 20:13, 21:25-26, 24:33-34

_____

_____

_____

_____

_____

_____

4. What blessings come as a result of diligence?

Prov. 10:4, 10:16, 12:11, 12:14, 12:24, 13:11, 14:23, 15:19, 21:5, 22:29, 28:19

_____

_____

_____

_____

_____

_____

5. How should Christian servants relate to Christian masters? How should Christian servants relate to unbelieving masters?

1 Cor. 4:2; Eph. 6:5-8; Col. 3:22-24; 1 Tim. 6:1-2; Tit. 2:9-10; 1 Pet. 2:18-20

_____

_____

_____

_____

_____

6. Whose servant are you, ultimately?

Ps. 119:91; Rom. 6:1-23; 1 Cor. 7:22-23; Col. 3:22-24; 1 Pet. 2:16

_____

_____

7. How can you apply the biblical principles above in your relationships with your boss, your fellow workers, and the customers you serve?

_____

_____

_____

_____

_____

_____

_____

_____

Examine Yourself:

1. Are you diligent in the tasks you are given now by parents, teachers, bosses, or other authorities?

2. Do you ever make excuses to get out of work?

3. Do you finish tasks on time?

4. Are you cheerful in your work?

5. How much education or training does your chosen career require?

6. What part of this necessary training do you still need to get?

7. Does this career require any licensing or certification?

8. Do you need a college degree?

9. How much will it cost, and how will you pay for it?

10. Will your parents help you pay for it?

11. Can you learn any of the necessary skills from parents, friends, or other people you know?

12. Can you work along side or apprentice with an experienced man to prepare yourself, or at least to get part of your training?

13. Will the skills you learn be applicable to other jobs/careers if you ever have to change work?

14. Do you have skills in another type of work that could bring in extra income or help you find work if you were no longer able to work in the area you are pursuing now?

15. At what point in your career or career preparation do you need to move out of your parents' home? How will this affect you and them? Have you discussed this with them?

Hear Counsel:

- Once you have chosen your career direction, you should set some specific goals and work towards those goals. Pursuing your career will probably include finishing your education, getting work experience, and getting established as an employee or a business owner.

- If you haven't made a habit of working hard and working cheerfully, you need to start right now! No matter what career you choose, cheerful diligence will play a huge part in your success. According to Proverbs, one of the best ways to get a job promotion is to be diligent and faithful.

- Parents: in order for your sons to learn diligence, they need to have meaningful work and responsibilities in the home, even at a young age.

- Learn to work hard, focus, and persevere during this time.

- Learn MORE THAN ONE SKILL – that way, you will be a better provider no matter what happens.

- Have lots of skills and lots of tools.

- Completing a college degree will not make you automatically successful. If you are in college, you should be there for a specific reason. Know what you are pursuing this training for! Evidence proves that college students with a vision generally do much better than students who are still trying to choose their direction.

- Getting vocational education and working while still living with your parents, when possible, will allow you to save more money.

- Being occupied with hard work is a good thing, especially as a young man.

- If starting your own business, don't spend money that you didn't earn in that field, and don't borrow money to get started. Most businesses that fail in the first year do so because their owners start out big with borrowed money and no experience. If you grow gradually, only spending what your business earns, you will be wiser and more experienced as you take on greater expenses to expand the business. (From Gregg Harris in the **Home and Family Business Workshop**.)

- Much of what the Bible says to servants is applicable both to employees, who serve their bosses, and to self-employed men, who serve their customers.

Take Action:

1. Give your very best to whatever work or study you are committed to at present. In what ways can you do better? Do you think you are being lazy in any part of your work or study?

2. Ask your parents to evaluate your work habits. How can you do better?

3. Consider these different methods for getting your career training:

   - Enter an apprenticeship, internship, or any other agreement to work with or learn from a skilled man that you know.

- Learn your parents' career from them, if their work fits your skills and interests.

- Start at a lower level in the field and work your way up as you learn through on-the-job training and grow in your abilities. (Use caution, and research your field to see if this is possible. This used to be very common, but it is not as easy today.)

- Attend a vocational school or traditional college campus, if it is affordable.

- Find correspondence courses, Internet-based classes, or other distance learning programs that will teach you the necessary skills and knowledge.

- Use a combination of the above methods.

4. If you know someone who does the work you are interested in, arrange a time to talk or work with him. See if he would be able to give you any training or work experience with him in the future. Ask him for counsel about further training you would need.

5. Find ways you can serve others that will employ skills you hope to use in your career, like helping with music for your church or helping others with building projects.

6. Talk with your parents. Discuss the different options for getting education and experience in the area you are pursuing.

7. Talk with your parents about paying for your higher education. Discuss ways you could earn money to pay your way. Ask them how much they think you should pay and how much they are willing to pay for you.

8. List some ways you could earn money to pay your way in any special training you need.

9. Pray for diligence, strength, and perseverance as you pursue your career.

10. Pray that God will bring opportunities your way that will help you get your training and get established in your career.

For Further Study:

1. Read **Preparing Sons to Provide for a Single-Income Family**, by Steven Maxwell. Parents and young men alike will find this to be a very helpful book. Besides giving specific directions for raising hard-working, productive boys, Mr. Maxwell reminds us that your **character** can make or break your career, no matter what skills or training you have.

2. Especially if you are considering any college studies, read **Accelerated Distance Learning**, by Brad Voeller, for practical and time-saving ideas for getting your college degree.

Vocation Resources

Your Career in Changing Times, by Lee Ellis and Larry
Burkett, published by Moody Publishers. *(6)*
Even though this book was written in the '90's, it still
offers much excellent counsel to anyone who wants to
make wise, godly career decisions. Another must-read!

Finding the Career That Fits You, by Lee Ellis and Larry
Burkett, published by Moody Publishers. *(6)*
This offers much of the same material as **Your Career in
Changing Times**, but in a workbook form. This book
would be especially helpful if you are still trying to determine your strengths and how to make use of them in a
career. A test is included to help you determine and
analyze your personality type according to the DISC
system.

The Best of the 2006 Entrepreneurial Bootcamp, produced
by Vision Forum. *(6, 10)*
Lectures on the importance of an entrepreneurial spirit
and much more practical advice for business owners,
business-starters, and employees who would serve their
masters well.

Finding a Job You Can Love, by Ralph Mattson and Arthur
Miller, published by P&R Publishing. *(3)*
Another book that can help you understand your inter-
ests and motivations and make godly career choices.

A Sacred Foundation, by Michael Farris and L. Reed Elam,
published by Loyal Publishing. *(3, 6, 7)*
Chapter 5, "Protection and Provision," describes the
husband's responsibility to provide for his family, along
with some of the common pitfalls and temptations to
failure in this responsibility.

Preparing Sons to Provide for a Single-Income Family, by
Steven Maxwell, published by Managers of Their Homes.
(9)
This is an excellent book for both fathers and young
men. Mr. Maxwell reminds us that character and heart
attitudes are the most decisive factor in our ability to
provide for a family, and he gives a great deal of practical, biblical advice for raising godly, hard-working sons.

Plants Grown Up, by Pam Forster, published by Doorposts. *(1,
5, 6, 7)*
For Bible studies and character training projects related
to vocational preparedness, see the following chapters:
    "Faithfulness in Performing a Job"
    "Perseverance in Trials"
    "Finishing What We Start"
    "Conquering Laziness"

Accelerated Distance Learning, by Brad Voeller, published by
Global Learning Strategies. *(3, 6, 10)*
This book provides a helpful, no-nonsense perspective
for any young man who is pursuing a college degree, or
even just a few college classes. Learn how to speed up
your learning, save money, and get what you really need
to get established in your career field.

Home and Family Business Workshop, audio lectures by
Gregg Harris. *(Available from Charity Ministries:
www.charityministries.org/tapeministry)*
Helpful advice from an experienced home-business
launcher.

Vocation Notes:

_____

_____

_____

_____

_____

_____

_____

_____

_____

_____

_____

_____

_____

_____

_____

_____

_____

_____

_____

_____

_____

_____

_____

Vocation Goals:

_____

_____

_____

_____

_____

_____

_____

_____

_____

_____

_____

_____

_____

_____

_____

_____

_____

_____

_____

_____

CHAPTER 4
FINANCES

*Honor the LORD with thy substance, and with the
firstfruits of all thine increase: So shall thy barns be filled
with plenty, and thy presses shall burst out with new wine.
Proverbs 3:9-10*

*He that gathereth by labor shall increase.
Proverbs 13:11b*

*Better is a little with the fear of the LORD than great
treasure and trouble with it.
Proverbs 15:16 (ESV)*

*Give me neither poverty nor riches; feed me with food
convenient for me.
Proverbs 30:8b*

Foolish money management has been the downfall of many young
men, and a high percentage of marriage problems are related to
money problems as well. Young men desperately need to grow in
wisdom in this area! The Bible is full of principles related to money,
and the book of Proverbs, especially, contains practical advice to
young men about the wise use of money. Don't ignore this wisdom!

Give God His Tithe

Study Scripture:

1. Was tithing practiced before the Mosaic law was given?

Gen. 14:18-20, 28:20-22

_____

_____

_____

2. What part of our wealth should we give to God?

Ex. 23:19a; Lev. 27:30-32; Deut. 14:22; Prov. 3:9

_____

_____

3. What uses of the tithe are mentioned in God's law?

Num. 18:21; Deut. 14:22-23

_____

_____

_____

_____

4. Does God command us to give to the poor?

Deut. 15:11; Luke 18:22; Gal. 2:9-10

_____

5. What does God promise to those who obey His commands to give?

Ps. 41:1; Prov. 3:9-10, 19:17, 22:9, 28:27; Mal. 3:8-10; Luke 6:38; Mark 10:21

_____

_____

_____

6. What happens to those who intentionally neglect the poor?

Prov. 21:13, 28:27

_____

_____

7. What else does Jesus say about giving?

Matt. 5:42, 6:1-4, 25:31-46; Mark 10:17-27; Luke 12:33-34

_____

_____

_____

_____

Examine Yourself:

1. Do you give God a tithe (10%) of all of your increase (profit)?

2. Why or why not?

3. What opportunities do you have for other giving beyond the tithe? Think of particular church ministries, missions, charities, and people in need that you could contribute to.

1. How much do you give to these causes in a year? Can you budget a certain amount or percentage of your earnings for other giving besides the tithe?

5. Do you tithe before or after taxes?

6. Do you expect to always be repaid for your giving, or do you trust God and continue to give, even when you don't see direct blessings?

Hear Counsel:

- Parents, you can teach your children financial responsibility with their allowance or earnings. Instill tithing habits at an early age to remind them that our money is God's.

- Make a consistent habit of tithing, and make other offerings besides. Be grateful for God's blessings.

- Remember that all your money is God's money, and he has made you a steward of it.

- The church as a whole could have a much greater impact on our society if Christians would obey God and give at least the tithe.

- Money mainly needs to be kept in the right context. Getting money is good, as long as 1) you are not greedy, 2) it doesn't control all your time, 3) you don't sin to get it, 4) you use it benevolently, and 5) you remember that it doesn't last.

- When your income increases, view this as an opportunity to give more, not just a chance to raise your standard of living. Be grateful for God's blessings!

- How a young man deals with material possessions and money can be a good indicator of his approach to life in general.

Take Action:

1. Budget 10 percent of your present income for tithe.

2. Budget an additional percentage to go to charity, missions, care of the elderly, sponsoring the care of an orphan, etc.

3. Pray that God will provide for your needs even when you are giving him a tenth of your income.

4. Talk with your parents or other adults and ask them how they have seen God's blessing or cursing based on people's commitment to tithing and giving.

For Further Study:

1. For a more complete discussion of tithing and giving from a Scriptural standpoint, read chapters 12-15 in **Money, Posessions, and Eternity**, by Randy Alcorn.

Be a Wise Steward

Study Scripture:

1. What Biblical principles should encourage us to have a budget?

Ps. 112:5; Prov. 21:29, 24:27, 27:12; Luke 14:28-32

_____

_____

Examine Yourself:

1. Do your parents use a budget?

2. Do you know how it is organized?

3. Have you used a budget before? Was it helpful?

4. How do you make decisions about how to spend and save your money?

5. Do you spend money on things you can't afford?

6. Do you make purchases impulsively or after careful consideration?

7. Do you know how much you spend a month on transportation? Insurance? Clothes? Entertainment? Giving?

Hear Counsel:

- Know how to budget. Most people need a budget plan.

- Budgeting is a good tool to help you control and prioritize the use of your money. Put basic necessities like food, clothing, shelter, and giving first, and then make wise use of what remains.

- Budgeting is most necessary for those who spend easily. A couple that spends little may be able to do without a budget if they both have good saving and spending habits.

- A budget can help you save money.

- A budget plan can help you avoid going into debt buying things you can't afford.

- Fathers — you can train your sons to have good budgeting habits by imposing a system of budget categories for their earnings or allowance when they are young.

- Know what it will cost to support a household, and make plans for earning enough money to consistently pay for necessities. You need to have the costs of living covered by your income, or it will be very hard to keep your wife at home and stay out of debt.

- Housing will most likely take a large percentage of your budget. (See the later section on housing, pages 107-111.)

Take Action:

1. Pray for wisdom to manage your money wisely.

2. Read sections 9-12 on budgeting in **The Complete Financial Guide for Young Couples** (pages 51-95).

3. Ask your parents to explain their budget plan. Can you set up something similar? How will yours be different now? How would it be different if you were married?

4. Record all your income and expenses for several months, or even for a whole year. Use the budget chart on page 210 to categorize your earning and spending, and discuss this with your parents. Are there any changes you should make for future months/years? Set up a revised budget plan using the budget chart, and then be faithful to your commitments.

5. Start your own checking account, if you don't already have one. Keep your checkbook balanced.

6. Set up a notebook with ledger pages to record your current income, spending, and other money management.

7. Using the budget chart on page 210, prepare your own budget plan for a young husband and wife.

8. Conduct a "cost of living" survey. If you need help, ask your parents to help you find the prices of housing, heating and water bills, insurance, auto expenses, and food costs in today's prices (use the form on page 209). After you have filled in this survey, show it to other couples you know and ask them how their budget compares. They may have some helpful suggestions for you.

For Further Study:

1. Complete **The Mathematics of Budgeting** from the "Mathematics for Everyday Living" series.

2. Before you are married, set up budget categories for the main expenses you will have like housing, insurance, etc., and save money in these categories.

Save For the Future

Study Scripture:

1. Is it wise to save up towards future needs?

Prov. 6:6-8, 21:20, 27:12; Gen. 41

_____

_____

2. What do the following verses teach about planning?

Prov. 16:1-9, 19:21, 21:31

_____

_____

3. Should we trust in our savings for protection from troubles? What else should we "store up" besides money?

Ps. 62:10b; Prov. 11:28, 16:8; Matt. 6:19-21; 1 Tim. 6:6-19

_____

_____

_____

Examine Yourself:

1. Have you saved any of your earnings so far?
2. What are some good reasons for saving money?
3. Are you living in a self-disciplined, sacrificial way right now? Are you living frugally in order to save for future needs of your family?

4. Are you being a good steward of whatever financial bless-ings God has given you?

5. What things do you spend your money on right now?

6. How do you plan to support yourself and your wife in your old age?

7. Do you desire to be able to give an inheritance to your children or grandchildren?

8. How would you picture your "retirement"?

9. Do you ultimately trust God to protect and provide for you and your future family, even as you plan and save for the future?

10. Do you have a plan for financial setbacks? What would you do if you had to be unemployed for a time, or if you had a large, unexpected expense?

Hear Counsel:

- Before marriage, earn lots of money, and don't spend it un-less you are investing for more gains. Don't just buy yourself expensive toys. There is never a better time to save, since as a young man you have very few expenses.

- Don't squander money on unnecessary toys – you aren't your own person. You can begin sacrificing for your wife and chil-dren now by not buying the expensive toys that men are tempted to have.

- Do buy tools or things you will need later. Invest in the fu-ture, and in education, skills, and tools that will help you earn long-term.

- Buying things you know you will need later may help save money in the long run. Keep your eye out for things that will appreciate in value.

- Learn basic skills that can save you money around the home.

- Entering marriage with some savings will free you from unnecessary pressures or emergencies.

- Start out your marriage with a pattern of economic living.

- Save for good reasons; don't just hoard.

- Having savings makes you better able to provide for your own family or help others in times of need.

- Be generous. There will be many small expenses (and some big ones) that will be worth it just to please your wife.

- Investing your time and energy (and your money) in your family will bring far greater returns, in God's eyes, than monetary savings or investments ever will.

- Always save something!

Take Action:

1. Start a savings account.

2. Begin saving a set percentage of your income for the future.

3. Using the budget chart (page 210), analyze your present spending and see if you are spending too much on unnecessary things. How much more could you save if you cut back in these areas?

4. List as many things as you can think of that will help you save money right now.

5. Make a list of things you could do to save money when you are married (think of house repairs, auto maintenance, etc.). Work with your parents or others to learn some of these skills as soon as you can.

6. List some specific things that you can save for now that will help you and your wife when you are married.

7. Begin saving a set percentage of your income for a dowry (see Chapter 5, pages 115-125).

8. Ask your parents or other people you respect about options for saving and investing. Get their advice for how you should

save and invest both now and later on in your life.

9. Read "Part 2 – Critical Family Issues" and "Part 4 – Ten Keys to Successful Investing," in **The Complete Financial Guide for Young Couples**, by Larry Burkett.

10. Pray for the necessary self-discipline and wisdom to save your money at the right times and for the right goals.

For Further Study:

1. Complete **The Mathematics of Saving** and **The Mathematics of Investing** from the "Mathematics Everyday Living" series.

2. Search for the best interest rate available for a savings account or for a certificate of deposit.

3. Talk with someone who understands different types of investing, and ask them questions. What are the advantages and disadvantages of investing in stocks and mutual funds? What risks are involved? Why is a "diversified portfolio" important? How should your investment strategy change as you move through different stages of life?

4. If you or your parents are self-employed, there may be opportunities for investing that will be better than most banking options. Invest a portion of your savings in a part of this business, with a plan for getting that money back within a set time period.

Avoid Debt

Study Scripture:

1. How does the Bible portray borrowing?

Deut. 28:2-12, 28:44-45

_____

_____

2. What has a borrower essentially become?

Prov. 22:7; Matt. 18:25-26

_____

_____

_____

3. Is it wrong for Christians to be servants? Is it better to be free?

1 Cor. 7:20-24

_____

_____

4. How could the servitude of debt become a problem for a Christian?

Deut. 6:5; Luke 16:13

_____

_____

5. What is another reason not to borrow?

Prov. 27:1; James 4:13-15

_____

_____

6. Is it wise to co-sign for another person's borrowing?

Prov. 6:1-5, 11:15, 17:18, 22:26-27

_____

7. How should Christians lend?

Ex. 22:25-27; Lev. 25:35-37; Deut. 15:1-11, 23:19-20; Luke 6:34-36

_____

_____

_____

Examine Yourself:

1. Have you ever borrowed money? What were the results? Why did you decide to borrow? Was this a good reason?

2. Have you ever known anyone else who borrowed money? What were the results? Why did they decide to borrow?

3. When do you think borrowing would be permissible for a Christian?

4. What are some disadvantages of borrowing?

5. Do you understand different types of interest rates?

6. Do you understand how a mortgage works? How does the down payment amount affect the monthly payment amount? What determines the monthly payment amount?

Hear Counsel:

- Borrowing should be generally avoided, and in most cases it is extremely foolish, but it is not always a sin.

- A young man should be financially independent before entering into marriage.

- Borrowing is presuming on the future and on God's provision. You don't know that you will be able to repay a debt.

- Borrowing makes it harder for us to give generously to others.

- Borrowing essentially makes you a slave to your creditors. You are under obligation to them until you have paid everything back, and this will limit your ability to serve God with your time and money.

- Oftentimes, borrowing is telling God that we know better what we need than He does, and that we think He is not adequately providing for us.

- If you save up to buy something instead of borrowing, often you will realize that you don't really need it, or that it really isn't worth spending the money on.

- Don't use credit cards (unless the balance is faithfully paid off every month)! If you are very self-disciplined, credit cards can be a useful tool to boost your credit for buying a house; even then, they must be used very carefully.

- Don't borrow, except possibly for a house if it is the only way to buy and you can pay it off in a reasonable time. Borrow only with wisdom, with progress in mind.

- Borrowing for a house is different than most kinds of borrowing, since a house is more likely to keep its value.

- Avoid borrowing for something that does not back itself up. (Houses will most likely keep their value or increase in value, while cars will decrease in value.)

- Don't ever take out the biggest mortgage you can make payments on. For example, figure the highest 15-year mortgage you can afford, and then get a 30-year mortgage for that amount instead. Then, you can still pay the 15-year payment, and you will have more flexibility if your financial situation changes (you can always back off and just pay the 30-year payments). You will also save enormous amounts of interest!

Take Action:

1. Complete **The Mathematics of Borrowing** from the "Mathematics for Everyday Living" series, especially chapter 4, "Home Mortgages." This chapter will introduce you to the basics of home mortgages and show ways you can save money, like making a larger downpayment, adding to your monthly payments, and comparing the cost of renting vs. buying to make the best choice.

2. Read John Thompson's article **Owe No Man: The Discipline of Debt-Free Living**, and discuss it with your parents. Discuss with your parents or other adults the scriptural principles for borrowing in today's culture. When is borrowing sinful for the Christian? In what circumstances is borrowing permissible?

3. Pray for wisdom to borrow only when necessary and to avoid any sinful borrowing, now and in the future.

For Further Study:

1. Read "Part 4, Borrowing and Lending," in **Using Your Money Wisely**, by Larry Burkett.

2. List some ways you could buy a house someday without borrowing. (Some ideas are listed at the end of John Thompson's article.)

3. Find out how much the value of a new car depreciates as soon as you drive it off the lot.

Pay Your Taxes

Study Scripture:

1. What did Jesus say about paying taxes?

Matt. 17:24-27, 22:16-21; Luke 3:12-13

_____

_____

_____

Examine Yourself:

1. Are Christians required to pay taxes?

2. Why or why not?

3. What taxes have you had to pay so far?

Hear Counsel:

- Pay your taxes! Our country's taxes are excessive, but not as bad as they were in the days when Jesus told His disciples to "Render unto Caesar the things that are Caesar's."

Take Action:

1. Find the requirements for filing a tax return.

2. Prepare and file a tax return for your earnings each year (if you meet the earning requirements). If you don't need to file a return yet, help your father file his tax return.

3. Talk to your parents and other men to get some ideas of how you can get legitimate tax deductions and credits.

4. Find out how being married, having children, and having a house can effect your taxes.

5. Pray that God will provide for you as you pay your taxes honestly.

For Further Study:

1. Complete **The Mathematics of Taxes** from the "Mathematics Everyday Living" series.

2. Find out how the employee and the self-employed person must pay taxes differently.

Use Insurance Wisely

Study Scripture:

1. Should we have a plan, as husbands and fathers, for caring for our family in an emergency?

Prov. 22:3, 27:1; 1 Tim. 5:8

_____

_____

_____

2. Should we trust our insurance to protect us?

Prov. 21:31; Is. 31:1

_____

_____

3. Should we pay, either directly or through an insurance plan, for accidents we cause and services we receive?

Ex. 21:18-19, 21:30-36; Lev. 24:18; Ps. 37:21

_____

_____

_____

Examine Yourself:

1. Have you paid any insurance yet?

2. What types of insurance do your parents have?

3. What types of insurance do you think it is prudent to have?

4. Do you know what an average visit to a doctor's office costs? Do you know what a visit to the emergency room costs?

5. Can you discipline yourself to put money aside for smaller expenses and emergencies that might otherwise require insurance (like routine health care)?

6. Would you be able to pay the bill if you had a medical emergency that required hospitalization? How much would be covered by insurance?

7. How does being self-employed or being an employee affect your insurance planning?

8. Do you trust your insurance to protect you from problems, or do you ultimately trust God to protect you and to always do what is best for you?

Hear Counsel:

- It is foolish and almost impossible to go without some kind of insurance in today's society. You really need to have insurance if you are going to protect and provide for your family.

- At least have a low premium, high deductible insurance policy to cover huge medical expenses. One hospital stay or an operation without insurance coverage could put you in debt for the rest of your life.

- Young men should research the costs for a family's routine health care, simple visits to the doctor, hospital stays, and common surgery procedures. This reality check will help you make wise decisions about your insurance.

- Car insurance is required to have a driver's license.

- You should have some kind of life insurance once you are married. This is one way you can ensure that your wife is provided for. (Life insurance accomplishes one of the purposes of the dowry — see Chapter 5.)

Take Action:

1. Read section 16, "Insurance" (pages 128-139), in **The Complete Financial Guide for Young Couples**, by Larry Burkett.

2. Describe how the following insurance plans operate, and define the following terms:

   > Term life insurance
   >
   > Whole life/permanent life insurance
   >
   > Premium
   >
   > Deductible
   >
   > HSA (Health savings account)
   >
   > PPO (Preferred provider organization)
   >
   > HMO (Health maintenance organization)
   >
   > HRA (Health reimbursement account)
   >
   > Christian sharing plans
   >
   > Catastrophic insurance

3. Ask your parents about the insurance that they pay right now for home, car, and health. What company provides the insurance? How much does it cost per year? What benefits would it provide if needed?

4. Decide which types of insurance are necessary, and which ones are more optional. With the counsel of your parents and other experienced adults, decide what kind of coverage you will need for your family in the future. Talk to adults or call some insurance companies to get an idea of what this will cost, and use these figures when completing your cost of living survey and budget plan (pages 209-210).

5. Do some research and decide if it is better to pay a higher premium and have a lower deductible amount, or if you should pay a lower premium and have a high deductible. What factors might influence this decision?

6. If your age and level of income allows, start paying some of your own insurance, like car, medical, or dental insurance.

7. Pray for God's protection on you and your future family. Pray that you will be able to provide for your future family and their medical needs.

For Further Study:

1. Complete **The Mathematics of Insurance** from the "Mathematics Everyday Living" series.

2. Read the section titled "Insurance — is it Scriptural?" on pages 98-100 in **Using Your Money Wisely**, by Larry Burkett.

Provide Housing and Transportation

Study Scripture:

1. Will God provide for our needs if we are obedient to him?

Ps. 37:23-25; 1 Tim. 6:6-8

_____

_____

2. At the same time, what is one command God gives us in regard to our families?

1 Tim. 5:8

_____

_____

Examine Yourself:

1. Do you have a car yet? If so, how did you purchase it? How much does its upkeep and gas cost you each month?

2. Do you understand the general maintenance needs of a car?

3. Do you faithfully attend to these needs?

4. Will you have to get a different car when you are married? What about when you have children?

5. Have you considered buying a house?

6. Do you know the average cost of a house in your area?

7. Does renting or buying sound better to you? Why?

8. What kind of tasks are involved in maintaining your own home?

9. Do you actively assist in maintaining the home you live in now?

10. Will you have enough savings for a down payment on a house when you get married?

11. Do you think you could save enough to buy a house debt-free? (Some young men have done it!)

12. Do you have the skills, or know family or friends with the skills necessary to build a house? (This might help you save money or avoid borrowing.)

Hear Counsel:

▪ Housing and transportation are two of the largest expenses that every family must pay.

▪ Men can easily lust after fancy houses and cars, but we should instead glorify God by sticking to what we can afford that will best provide for our family. What goes on inside our houses is far more important than what the houses look like. Remember, housing and transportation are *tools!*

▪ Buying a new car is generally not wise (especially if you have to borrow to buy it). Besides, paying for repairs on a used car is often cheaper than making payments on a new one.

▪ In some situations, young men are able to save more money towards buying a house or car in the future by being patient about buying a car or moving out of their parents' home. If you are pursuing schooling or a vocation near your home, you should seriously consider avoiding these expenses when possible.

▪ Buying a home before your marriage can be a great blessing, but keep in mind that many things about a house will matter more to a wife than they will to you. Your home will be her primary "workplace" and area of dominion.

▪ Purchasing a home and/or land early on in your marriage can stabilize later years on a single income with children. Buying a house can help you provide for yourself and your family in the future. Homes are a good investment, but you will have to work harder to make time with your family. You may want to wait a few years before buying, or look for a house that doesn't take a lot of repairs or maintenance right away.

- Be careful about buying a house. Make sure it will not require too much of your time, energy, and money. Renting will give you more family time and fewer worries. Buying a house ties you down and uses up lots of time and money when they are most valuable to you. Buying is not always cheaper by the time you spend money on taxes, repairs, and utilities.

- Buying a house can be one of the best investments for building family wealth. Owning property will make it easier for you to provide for yourself and your wife in your old age, and it gives you more ability to bless your children with inheritances someday.

- If you want to buy a house that needs lots of work, think about waiting until you have some sons to help you. That way you can have family and teaching time instead of spending the time away from your family like you would if you bought such a house right after marriage.

Take Action:

1. Set goals now for how you will provide housing for your future family, and start working towards those goals.

2. Read the sections on housing and automobiles (pages 73-80) in **The Complete Financial Guide for Young Couples**, by Larry Burkett.

3. If you hope to buy a house someday, begin saving a percentage of your income now towards a down payment.

4. Pray for God's help as you make plans to provide housing and transportation for your family. Pray that he will give you wisdom and that he will provide for your family's needs. Pray that he will be preparing and leading you to the best housing op-

tions for your family in the future.

5. Talk to men you know who have either bought or rented property. Ask them about the advantages or disadvantages of each option. Ask about differences in taxes, insurance costs, and responsibilities.

6. If possible, make the choice to live with your parents longer while you pursue schooling, vocational training, and work, so that you will be able to save money for the future, or at the very least avoid going into debt for your education.

7. Make the choice to live with a simple, functional car, or delay buying one until you truly need it, and put aside any saved money for future housing or transportation.

8. Research each of the following car maintenance tasks:

    Lubrication
    Changing the oil
    Replacing transmission fluid
    Checking brakes
    Replacing brakes
    Checking tires
    Replacing tires
    Visual inspection
    Washing

    For each item on this list, find out how often it must be done, why it must be done, and how to do it. (You might want to ask an auto mechanic for help in answering these questions.) Who must perform each of these tasks? Find out which ones you can do and which ones you will have to take to a shop. For those you can do yourself, begin doing them for your own car or helping your father do them for your family's car. Make a maintenance calendar for this car and perform regular maintenance based on this schedule from now on.

9. Study the workings of home mortgages and learn how you can save money if you must borrow to buy a house someday.

10. Find out what other costs are involved in buying a house besides the initial down payment and monthly mortgage payments.

11. Do some research and find out what it costs for different housing options in your area. How much does it cost to rent an apartment? A duplex or condominium? A house? How much does it cost to purchase an apartment, duplex, condominium, or house?

For Further Study:

1. Talk with your father, and perhaps with other men you know, and make an "essential tool list" of the tools that you will need when you start your own household. (You can also see my list on page 211.) How many of these tools do you already have? If there are tools you know you will still need, buy them for yourself, or put them on your wish list for Christmas or birthday gifts.

2. If you know anyone who is familiar with or works in the real estate business, ask them for advice on the above questions. Ask them for counsel on when and why you should buy or rent a house.

3. Think of the other considerations (besides cost) involved in finding suitable housing in your first years of marriage. What size of living space do you need? What location do you want to live in? Do you want to be in the city or in the country? What type of utilities do you need?

4. If you ever consider buying a house, first consider the amount of work involved in any repairs that need to be made. How much of your family time will it take?

5. Review the previous section, "Avoid Debt" (pages 97-100).

Finance Resources

The Complete Financial Guide for Young Couples: A Lifetime Approach to Spending, Saving and Investing, by Larry Burkett, published by Cook Communications Ministries. *(3)*
Practical advice based on Biblical principles and years of counseling experience. This book can help you make plans now and avoid many common money problems in your future marriage. Highly recommended!

Using Your Money Wisely, by Larry Burkett, published by Moody Press. *(3)*
Examines Scriptural principles related to anything that involves money, including business, the church, and the family.

How to Manage Your Money: An In-Depth Bible Study on Personal Finances, by Larry Burkett, published by Moody Press. *(3)*
A fill-in-the-blanks study on Christian money management.

Biblical Economics, A Commonsense Guide to Our Daily Bread, by R. C. Sproul Jr., published by the Highlands Study Center. *(6, 8)*
A simple but pointed study in economics from a sound biblical perspective.

Money, Posessions, and Eternity, by Randy Alcorn, published by Tyndale House. *(3)*
A detailed study of Scriptural principles for managing our money and possesions for God's glory.

"Owe No Man: The Discipline of Debt-Free Living," article by John Thompson. *(Available at www.christiancourtship.com)*

The Mathematics for Everyday Living series, published by Meridian Creative Group. *(Unfortunately, this series is out of print, but you can check Amazon.com for availability)*

> **The Mathematics of Budgeting**
>
> **The Mathematics of Saving**
>
> **The Mathematics of Buying**
>
> **The Mathematics of Inflation and Depreciation**
>
> **The Mathematics of Borrowing**
>
> **The Mathematics of Investment**
>
> **The Mathematics of Insurance**
>
> **The Mathematics of Taxes**
>
> These practical books serve as a great introduction to many basic financial skills.

Finance Notes:

_____

_____

_____

_____

_____

_____

_____

_____

Finance Goals:

_____

_____

_____

_____

_____

_____

_____

_____

_____

_____

CHAPTER 5

DOWRY

*And Jacob loved Rachel; and said, I will serve thee seven
years for Rachel thy younger daughter.
And Jacob served seven years for Rachel; and
they seemed unto him but a few days,
for the love he had to her.
Genesis 29:18, 20*

*Husbands, love your wives, even as Christ also loved the
church, and gave himself for it.
Ephesians 5:25*

It is possible that many of you who read this book have never
heard of a dowry. Or, at least, you never thought of continuing
this practice in today's culture. However, the dowry (or bride-
price) is mentioned several times in the Bible, and it was even
included in the laws given to Israel in the Old Testament. Since
the practice is mentioned in the Bible, and since it has been practiced for the greater part of history in many cultures, we should
spend some time studying it.

First of all, what is a dowry? There are actually three terms, each with different meanings, related to this cultural practice. The word "dowry," in most cultures, refers to *wealth that the bride brings into the marriage* (the dowry was usually provided by her parents). The "bride-price," on the other hand, was *wealth that the groom gave to the bride's family*. A third term, "dower," has also been used in reference to w*ealth that a groom bestows on his bride*, either by giving it at their marriage, or by leaving it to her at his death. Maybe it is just because the King James Bible uses the word "dowry," but most of the men I have talked to and the books I have read use the term "dowry" as a general term referring to wealth brought into the marriage, whether it comes from the bride, the groom, or their families.

What was the dowry system for? Although it is not fully explained in the Bible, the practice mentioned in the Old Testament accomplished several things. In reading about this practice and talking to others who have studied it, I found the following purposes mentioned:

- It protected a wife in the event of her husband's death, abandonment, or apostasy.

- It proved the seriousness of prospective bridegrooms.

- It served as a screening device — it demonstrated a young man's ability to think ahead, earn and save money, and provide for a family, and it was one way for him to show his love for his future wife.

- The bridegroom showed his submission to the bride's father by providing the bride price that he required.

- It enriched the wife for dominion in her sphere – the home.

- In Old Testament culture, it was part of the system of inheritance.

One of the main goals of the dowry system was to bless and protect the bride, and this is still a worthy goal, especially as we seek to imitate Jesus and His love for us. In this chapter, it is this goal that we will seek to revive. Consequently, from here on I will use the term "dowry" to refer to the following: *Some form of wealth saved by a young man and given to his bride as a means of proving his preparedness and love, providing for her needs, and empowering her for dominion.*

Should the dowry still be *required* in today's culture? Christian pastors and writers seem to agree that grooms are no longer bound by Scripture to provide a dowry. In **Tools of Dominion**, Gary North argues that civil laws and functions of the Church now accomplish the main purposes behind the dowry as mentioned in the Old Testament. Also, sons and daughters in our culture usually share inheritance and responsibility for aged parents equally, so the system of dowry and bride price is no longer needed as part of the inheritance system.

Still, there are many good reasons to revive this practice in Christian marriages today:

- If you are a young man, saving a dowry can help you prepare for marriage, and giving a dowry is one way to show that you value and love your future bride.

- If you are a parent, teaching your young boys about the dowry can be a starting point for teaching them about godly courtship and marriage, and asking your daughter's potential suitors to provide a dowry will help test their preparedness and commitment.

- If you are a young lady, a dowry can help better prepare your future husband for your marriage, and if you are a wife, a dowry will help protect and provide for you and/or your descendants in the future.

Even if we decide not to give a dowry, we *are* still bound to fulfill some of the purposes of the dowry, even if we do this through other means (like providing emergency provision through a life insurance policy).

Understand Dowry Principles

Study Scripture

1. What did the groom give as a bride price in the following instances?

Gen. 29:15-30; Josh. 15:16-17; 1 Sam. 18:25-27; 1 Pet. 1:17-19

_____

_____

_____

_____

2. What is given to the bride as a dowry in the following verses?

Gen. 24:22; Ezek. 16:8-14

_____

_____

_____

3. In the Bible, who determined whether a bride price was required, and what it would be?

Gen. 34:8-12; 1 Sam. 17:25, 18:25-27

_____

_____

_____

4. How was the bride price used as a penalty for certain crimes?

Ex. 22:16-17

_____

_____

_____

_____

Examine Yourself:

1. Have you heard of a dowry before?

2. Do you know anyone who has given, or plans to give a dowry?

3. In what ways could you provide for your wife's future protection in the event that you die or become disabled?

4. Fathers: Do you plan to require a dowry for your daughters? In what situations would you choose to require or not require a dowry?

5. Young men: Do you plan to give a dowry to your future wife? Will you be prepared to provide a dowry if her father requires it?

6. What is the bride price that Christ gave for the Church? What can you learn from this for your own marriage?

Hear Counsel:

Why Should Young Men Have a Dowry?

- A dowry is one way to love as Christ loved. "Husbands, love your wives, as Christ loved the Church, and gave himself for her" (Eph. 5:25, ESV). Working hard, saving, and sacrificing some of your pleasures for your future wife, even before you know her, is a very good way to show Christ's love. It is also a good way for you to start learning to love her in your marriage.

- A dowry gives your wife a sense of worth, knowing that you worked hard for her. It gives her honor and shows that you value her. She can think back on all the time you spent working and saving, and she will know that you value her highly.

- By teaching sons to save for a dowry, fathers can also begin training boys about godly courtship at an early age. All young men need to learn early on that they must not "go courting" before their vocation is in place.

- Saving for a dowry, even at a young age, provides a reminder and motivation for boys to use their time, money, and energy wisely.

- A dowry demonstrates a young man's ability to provide for a wife and family. If he can accumulate a good amount of savings before marriage, it is a good indication that he is capable of earning a consistent wage that will support a family.

- A dowry demonstrates a young man's ability to earn, save, and plan for the future. It is a good exercise in self-discipline and wise money management.

- Having a dowry can help a young man demonstrate his honest intention of pursuing marriage.

- A dowry provides emergency provision/life insurance. Part of your dowry should include having a life insurance policy that would support your wife and children if you die.

- A dowry empowers your wife for dominion in the household. She can use it to start her own home-based business, or to buy tools to keep the household running.

- A dowry may be employed in purchasing, setting up, or beautifying the home. Your dowry savings may be the biggest amount of savings you have. You and your wife might agree to use it as a down payment on a house so that you can get established with less debt.

What Can I Give as a Dowry?

What you actually have as a dowry might vary greatly depending on the particular vocational path you are taking. A couple of these things could not be *given* literally, but they would still accomplish some of the goals of the dowry.

- Money. Depending on your situation, you may be able to accumulate 5, 10, 20, or 50 thousand dollars. With such large amounts of money, it is usually better to invest it and make it work for you than to let it sit in the bank. Thus, owning property or having a debt-free education might be even better than having a large amount of money saved.

- A house, land, or money for a down payment.

- A profitable, sustainable business, and the related tools.

- A debt-free education for a good career or trade. Getting your own education or getting established in a trade is not something that can be physically given to your wife, but it certainly shows that you are prepared to provide for her in the long-term.

- A life insurance policy (at least as part of a dowry).

- A monthly budget amount set aside for the wife to use however she wishes.

- The engagement and wedding rings might be considered part of the dowry. In today's culture, this may be all that remains of the original idea of dowry-giving.

- Gold and silver. This is one way you can invest part of your dowry. As a young boy I bought and received a few gold and silver coins, and they have increased in value over the years. Since your dowry savings may not be spent for many years, this is a pretty safe way to protect a portion of it. Gold and silver are substances of real value that will hold their value, often better than cash or even money in a savings account. My brothers and I have enjoyed handling some *real* money while collecting a few historic U.S. coins for our dowries. They used to be made of real gold and silver!

What Would a Wife Do With Dowry Money?

- Put it into savings and/or safe investments for the future.

- Save it to provide for herself and her family if the husband dies or becomes disabled.

- Save it for retirement or children's inheritance.

- Spend some of it on jewelry.

- Spend some of it on furniture or other items to beautify the new home and/or land.

- Spend some of it on home improvements (a kitchen remodel to accommodate better hospitality, for example).

- Spend some of it on other heirloom-quality things that will last her lifetime and perhaps be passed down to future generations.

- Invest it in her own home-business endeavors.

- Invest it in your business so that it can be more profitable and increase future provision.

- Invest some of it in additional training or education for herself.

- Help buy a house or land.

- Any other uses that she might think of that would glorify God, please her, or bless her family.

- Along with dowry money, the husband might include some instructions or suggestions — his written wishes as to how he would like the wife to use it. He might ask that she not spend any of it for a set amount of time; he might ask that she spend it only on things that are likely to hold or increase their value; he might ask that she spend a portion on furniture or jewelry; or he might recommend any other use that he thinks is wise. Still, the husband should not try to persuade his wife to spend her dowry on a particular thing or heavily influence what she does with it. The husband should make clear that all ownership and final decisions about using the dowry belong to his wife.

A Final Point of Counsel:

■ Whatever kind of dowry you decide to give or require, be sure you discuss it clearly with all who will be involved, since this practice is no longer part of our culture, and other Christians may have different ideas of what you mean by the term "dowry."

Take Action:

1. Talk to your parents and to some men in your church about giving a dowry. Do they think it is a good idea? Ask if they have ever heard of a dowry before, and if they have seen it used.

2. Pray that God will help you apply the principles of the dowry in your courtship and marriage.

3. Write down a plan of other ways you will accomplish the purposes of the dowry.

4. Research the terms "dowry," "dower," and "bride-price" at *www.wikipedia.org.*

5. Read "Chapter 9, How to Marry: The Betrothal Stage," from **God's Design for Scriptural Romance**, by John Thompson. In the section entitled "Applying Preparedness," Thompson has put together biblical teaching and further historical details of Hebrew culture to give a helpful explanation of the terms "dowry" and "bride-price." Give, in your own words, definitions of these two terms as they were used in biblical culture.

6. Research life insurance policies, and make a plan to have a life insurance plan as soon as you are married (see "Use Insurance Wisely," pages 103-106).

For Further Study:

1. Start saving for a dowry. From whatever you are earning, start saving at least 10 to 25 percent.

2. Make a savings plan for your dowry fund. Set a goal for a

minimum amount you want to have saved. How much can you put in your dowry each year? How many years will it take to reach your goal?

3. List some ways that you could invest some of your dowry funds at present.

4. Consider the different times that the dowry may be transferred: at engagement/betrothal, during the wedding, or over time after the wedding. What advantages or disadvantages do you see? What time do you think would be best?

5. Do some research on buying and selling gold and silver coins. How much of your savings should you put into gold or silver? Which one is better to get? Should you buy old coins or new bullion? Check the internet for silver and gold prices. Go to a coin shop and buy some gold or silver with part of your dowry savings.

Dowry Resources

Tools of Dominion (Chapter 6), by Gary North, published by
the Institute for Christian Economics. *(Available from
Amazon.com and www.garynorth.com)*
This commentary on the Old-Testament case laws is one
of the few books that addresses the dowry in much
detail. In chapter 6, Dr. North comments on Biblical
references to the dowry and fills in more details found by
studying other historical documents.

**God's Design for Scriptural Romance, Chapter 9: How to
Marry: The Betrothal Stage**, by John Thompson.
(www.christiancourtship.com)
This article includes a summarized explanation of the
terms "dowry" and "bride-price." John Thompson draws
on Scriptural references, scholarly articles, and com-
mentaries (including **Tools of Dominion**).

Dowry Notes:

_____

_____

_____

_____

_____

_____

_____

Dowry Goals:

_____

_____

_____

_____

_____

_____

_____

_____

_____

_____

Chapter 6

Courtship

Then the LORD God said, 'It is not good that the man should be alone; I will make him a helper fit for him.'
Therefore a man shall leave his father and his mother and hold fast to his wife, and they shall become one flesh.
Genesis 2:18 & 24 (ESV)

Hearken unto thy father that begot thee, and despise not thy mother when she is old.
Proverbs 23:22

Although it must come *after* our other preparations, Christian courtship is a vital part of preparing for marriage. In our courtships, we should do everything possible to build a strong foundation for a godly marriage. This stands in stark contrast to the world's way of dating, where young people act independently of authorities, follow their feelings, and learn to form and break multiple romantic relationships. This is practice for divorce, not for a lifelong marriage!

Not everyone agrees on the definition of the word "courtship," but it still may be the best word we have to refer to *a Bible-based pattern for pursuing marriage.* Unfortunately, a wide variety of practices have been labeled as "courtship" in today's Christian circles, so keep in mind that the word can mean different things to different people, and make sure that you share a similar definition of courtship with those you converse with (especially a potential wife and her family).

Although there are differences between various courtship methods, there are a few major principles that define the biblical courtship that Christians are attempting to recover:

1. Parents, as much as possible in each situation, exercise their proper authority and give counsel throughout the process, and sons and daughters honor this authority.

2. Young men and ladies do not pursue romantic relationships or enter courtship until they are sufficiently prepared for marriage.

3. Physical and emotional purity is carefully guarded and saved for the *one* person that you will marry.

4. Biblical principles are consciously sought and followed throughout the process. This includes understanding biblical manhood and womanhood, and Jesus' example of choosing, loving, and saving His bride, the Church.

By following these biblical principles, young men, you should be able to court and marry a wife in a manner that honors God and builds a strong foundation for your future marriage. It is important that you study these principles of courtship and discuss your vision with your parents before pursuing courtship. Even more importantly, parents should understand the principles of courtship and begin teaching these principles to their sons and daughters long before they are old enough to begin courting. Ideally, Christian children will grow up thinking, "Isn't this normal?"

Follow Biblical Principles

Study Scripture:

1. Who can give you a good wife?

Gen. 2:18; Ps. 84:11; Prov. 19:14; Rom. 8:28

_____

2. How did Adam find a wife? Why was he given a wife? What was Eve supposed to be for Adam?

Gen. 2:18-24

_____

_____

_____

3. How did Isaac find a wife?

Gen. 24

_____

4. How did Jacob find a wife? Did he follow his parents' counsel? Did he get counsel when arranging his marriage? What did he give as a dowry?

Gen. 28:1-9, 29:1-30

_____

_____

_____

_____

5. Did Esau honor his parents or ask for advice about his marriages?

Gen. 26:34-35, 28:8-9

---

6. How did Moses meet his wife? Who gave her to him?

Ex. 2:15-21

---

7. What was Samson's approach to getting a wife? Did he listen to his parents' advice? What happened?

Judg. 14:1-15:6, 16:1-31

---

8. How did Boaz find a wife? Why do you think his parents are not mentioned? Was he carried away by his emotions? Did Ruth listen to Naomi's advice?

Ruth 2-4

Examine Yourself:

1. What do your parents believe about dating, courtship, and betrothal? What are your beliefs?

2. Have you ever been involved in dating before?

3. Have you observed any form of Christian courtship before?

4. While growing up, how have you pictured finding a wife?

5. Are you exercising patience, waiting until you are truly ready for marriage before pursuing courtship?

6. How did your parents meet and get to know each other?

7. What kind of blessings or problems did they encounter?

8. Have any of your friends or siblings already been married?

9. What path to marriage did they take? What blessings or problems did they encounter?

10. Are you comitted to seeking counsel from your parents when the time comes for you to find a wife?

11. Are you prepared to submit yourself to the father of a young lady? Are you ready to be humble and teachable when you pursue courtship?

Hear Counsel:

- Don't get involved in romantic relationships with girls before you are ready for courtship and marriage.

- Know why you are pursuing marriage, and what marriage is before you move towards it.

- Don't pursue marriage when you are clearly not ready. Courtship is for finding a wife, not a "girlfriend."

- Purity includes your thoughts and emotions, not just your body.

- Since you (and your future wife) will never be *perfectly* prepared for marriage, you (and your parents) must determine when you are *sufficiently* prepared for marriage and ready to seek a wife. Trust God to lead you to your future spouse when you are ready, just as He did for Adam. Be assured that God will use marriage as He continues to sanctify both of you!

- Since marriage is a picture of Christ and His Bride, our approach to courtship should reflect our understanding of salvation. The young man should sacrifice, make his intentions plain, and put his own comfort and security on the line if necessary, rather than fishing around trying to discover the young lady's feelings before he commits himself.

- TRUST YOUR PARENTS. They know what is best for you, especially in relationships, and if you disregard their counsel in this area you will most certainly regret it later.

- Listen to your parents! They were your age once. They know you and have your best interests in mind. Wise parents will be preparing you for marriage from your earliest years, and they will know when you are sufficiently prepared. They will also have a better sense about what kind of young lady will be a good compliment and helper to you, and they will be able to spot character flaws that you might not notice before marriage. The counsel and opinions of peers should carry less weight than that of your parents. If you disregard your parents' counsel when you choose a wife, you will most likely regret it later.

- Parents MUST be involved in the courtship process, especially the parents of the young lady. If parents are not available, there should be some other godly adult to help guide the process and protect her.

- Having family members involved on both sides will make the true character of both young people plain, and deception and poor judgment will be diminished.

- Circumstances may dictate how long a courtship period lasts. The objectives should be to discern the true character and convictions of those involved, and to determine whether the two would be suitable spouses for each other.

- If at all possible, express your interest in a young lady to her father first. This protects her heart and allows her father to exercise his proper responsibility of protecting and guiding her.

- Be prepared to submit to the young lady's father. If he sets standards, do not try to go around him.

- PERSEVERE to win the father and the daughter. The courtship process may not be easy, but do not give up with his program! Fathers want their daughters married.

- Generally, young men need to exercise more self-control in the physical aspect of relationships.

Counsel For Fathers of Daughters:

- Evaluating a suitor takes wisdom! Work with your wife and daughter.

- Use wise judgment. No young man will be perfectly prepared in every way, but you must look for what is important.

- In evaluating a young man, look also at his family, and talk to others who know him.

- A young man's true character will be seen in how he acts within his own family.

- Keep in mind that young men may have problems acting normal around you if they know they're being evaluated.

- Watch out for big talkers who don't show any fruit.

- Consider character more of a deciding factor than other considerations.

- Look for good potential and hard-working habits. Finishing what is started shows responsibility.

- You should measure up to the standard you require of a suitor!

- If you plan to require a dowry, remember that situations will vary greatly, and a father must be wise in evaluating a young man's dowry. Each young man will have different opportunities and a different situation.

- Your daughter's husband should be able to continue the work you have begun in her.

- Girls are under their father's authority, and when they are married they switch to being under their husband's authority. They are never on their own.

Take Action:

1. Read **I Kissed Dating Goodbye**, by Joshua Harris, as an introduction to the idea of emotional purity before marriage.

2. Read **Courtship and Dating: So What's the Difference?**, by Dennis Gundersen, as an introduction to the idea of courtship.

3. Read chapters 17-19 in **The Family, God's Weapon for Victory**, by Robert Andrews.

4. Read **Her Hand in Marriage**, by Douglas Wilson. Summarize each chapter and discuss the content with your parents.

5. Pray that God will bring your future wife along at the right time, pray for peace about the issue until it is time, and pray that He will help you make wise decisions when you begin seeking a wife.

6. Talk with your parents about the vision they have for your courtship. How do they want you to find a wife? What part will they play in the process?

7. Talk with your parents about the goals you should reach before courtship. What do they want you to have in place before you pursue courtship and marriage? How will they help you reach these goals?

8. Make a list of goals you are committed to reaching before you consider courtship.

9. Write out the principles you want to follow for your own courtship.

10. Write out a specific plan to help you follow these principles.

(But keep in mind that God may bring along a different situation than you expect!)

For Further Study:

1. For a thorough study of Biblical principles relating to courtship and romance, read **God's Design for Scriptural Romance**, by John Thompson. I recommend using the study questions on pages 196-203, and, if you are a young man, discussing these articles with your parents.

2. Read chapter 5, "Preparing Your Child for Marriage," in **The Home Schooling Father**, by Michael Farris.

3. Ask married Christians that you know to tell you how they met each other.

4. Ask your parents about their approach to romance before marriage and the results.

5. Review the beliefs that you put in writing for action 5 from "Know What You Believe" in Chapter 1 (page 30). Think about which beliefs your wife must agree with you on. Are there any that she could disagree with you over?

Be Prepared to Recognize Your Helper

Study Scripture:

1. According to God's reasons for creating Eve, what purpose should a good wife have?

Gen. 2:18-24

_____

_____

2. What directions are given to wives in the New Testament?

Eph. 5:22-24; Col. 3:18; 1 Tim. 5:14; Tit. 2:4-5; 1 Pet. 3:1-6

_____

_____

_____

_____

3. What blessings should a godly wife bring her husband?

Ps. 128:3; Prov. 12:4, 14:1, 31:10-31; Tit. 2:4-5

_____

_____

_____

_____

4. What problems does a foolish wife bring on her husband?

Esth. 5:14, 7:9-10; Prov. 12:4, 14:1, 19:13, 21:9, 21:19, 27:15

_____

_____

_____

_____

5. What happened in the Bible when godly men married unbelieving wives?

Gen. 6:1-7; Judg. 3:5-8; 1 Kings 11:4; Neh. 13:25-27

_____

_____

_____

_____

6. What does the Bible say about Christians marrying unbelievers?

Deut. 7:3-4; Josh. 23:11-13; 1 Cor. 7:39; 2 Cor. 6:14-16

_____

_____

_____

Examine Yourself:

1. Is it all right to marry a non-Christian?

2. Are you committed to marrying a faithful Christian?

3. Why did God give Adam a wife?

4. What goals do you have for your own life and for your future family? (be specific)

5. How can a wife help you reach these goals? (be specific)

6. What is your understanding of a wife's role in the marriage and in the family?

7. What responsibilities do you expect your wife to carry in your family?

8. Do you trust your parents to give you good counsel regarding a prospective wife?

Hear Counsel:

- Trust God, in His sovereignty, to bring you the right young lady at the right time, as He did for Adam. Until then, keep working hard and preparing!

- You need to be the kind of person that the kind of person you want to marry would want to marry!

- Be sure that her convictions do not conflict with yours (be careful to distinguish between *convictions* and *preferences*).

- Observing a young lady's mother will often give you an idea of what kind of woman that young lady will become.

- Be careful not to have unreasonable expectations. Your wife will be a sinner just like you!

- Your parents can help you spot and avoid a contentious, brawling, or foolish woman.

- The woman you marry will have a huge effect on your family and your descendants for the rest of history. Just think about it! If you make a foolish choice and marry a foolish woman, your family could be destroyed. If you listen to wise counsel, have patience, and make a wise choice, marrying a wise woman who fears God, your descendants will be blessed for many generations! The Bible shows us that a whole nation can be destroyed if the men take ungodly wives (Gen. 6, Judg. 1-2).

Take Action:

1. Begin praying daily for your future wife, and for yourself, that you will both be well-suited to each other and prepared for your godly roles in your family. Pray also for her parents, that they would have wisdom in training and leading her and in protecting her heart.

2. Read Genesis 1-3 and Chapter 2, "The Family's Chief End," in **Bound for Glory**, by R. C. Sproul, Junior.

3. Read chapter 4, "It Is Not Good That Man Should Be Alone," in **The Family, God's Weapon for Victory**, by Robert Andrews. Also read chapter 9, "Imperishable Beauty – A Gentle and Quiet Spirit", chapter 10, "Homemaker – A Multi-Talented Professional", and chapter 11, "The Application of Proverbs 31 Today."

4. Write down the qualities and character that you see as important in your future wife. Discuss these with your parents.

For Further Study:

1. Complete the Bible studies in **Beauty and the Pig**, by Pam Forster, to gain a biblical perspective on true beauty.

2. List 5 people who could give you godly counsel regarding a prospective wife, and commit to asking them for counsel when the time comes.

Courtship Resources:

Note: You will find that each of these resources offers a slightly different perspective on courtship. No single book here describes exactly how our family has practiced or would practice courtship, but by reading several different books, you will begin to get an idea in your own mind of the vision you would like to follow with your own family. Try to read most of these books by the time you or your children are ready for courtship, and then agree with your family on the overall vision for courtship that you will carry into these years.

Number one resource: Your parents!

Number two resource: Other godly men and women, and your church leadership, especially those who have personally courted or guided their children in courtship already.

Courtship and Dating: So What's the Difference?, by Dennis Gundersen, published by Grace and Truth Books. *(7)* This short booklet serves as a great introduction to the foundational principles of Christian courtship.

I Kissed Dating Goodbye, by Joshua Harris, published by Multnomah Publishers. *(1, 3, 6, 7)* Another good introduction to courtship principles, especially if the idea is new to your family. This book focuses on the proper approach to romance, and the sin and temptation that permeates worldly dating. I would especially recommend this book to young men and women who will not be ready for courtship for several years.

Boy Meets Girl, by Joshua Harris, published by Multnomah Publishers. *(3, 6, 7)* After helping us protect hearts and refrain from romance in "I Kissed Dating Goodbye," Joshua Harris wrote a second book looking more deeply into courtship principles. After guarding your heart and preparing for marriage all these years, what do you do once you're really ready? This book will be helpful for parents and for young men and women who are prepared for marriage and ready to begin courting.

Her Hand In Marriage, by Douglas Wilson, published by Canon Press. *(1, 2, 3, 6, 7)*
A biblical model for courtship founded in a wise understanding of biblical marriage, manhood, and womanhood. Full of practical advice for parents and young people!

The Family, God's Weapon for Victory, by Robert Andrews, published by Sentinel Press (chapters 17-19). *(5, 6)*
Another excellent perspective on Christian courtship, emphasizing the responsibilities of fathers.

God's Design for Scriptural Romance, by John W. Thompson. *(Available from www.christiancourtship.com)*
An excellent biblical study on courtship principles, this will definitely stimulate your thinking on godly courtship. (I have provided study questions for you in Appendix B.)

Sex is Not the Problem, Lust Is (first printed as **Not Even a Hint**), by Joshua Harris, published by Multnomah Publishers. *(3, 6, 7)*
Encouragement, all based on Scripture, to help both young men and women fight temptations to lust.

Bound For Glory, by R.C. Sproul, Jr., published by Crossway Books. *(1, 3)*
Understand God's design for the family from the beginning of time.

To Have and to Hold, video message by "Little Bear" Wheeler. *(Available from Mantle Ministries: www.mantleministries.com/onlinestore)*
Exposes the extreme foolishness of modern dating and introduces Christian courtship as the alternative.

Beauty and the Pig, by Pam Forster, published by Doorposts. *(1, 5, 6)*
Ten Bible studies on godly beauty and how to recognize it.

Courtship Notes:

_____

_____

_____

_____

_____

_____

_____

_____

Courtship Goals:

_____

_____

_____

_____

_____

_____

_____

_____

_____

_____

_____

CHAPTER 7

FAMILY VISION

*Blessed is every one that feareth the LORD; that walketh
in his ways.
For thou shalt eat the labor of thine hands: happy shalt
thou be, and it shall be well with thee.
Thy wife shall be as a fruitful vine by the sides of thine
house: thy children like olive plants round about thy table.
Psalm 128:1-3*

*As for man, his days are like grass; he flourishes like a
flower of the field; for the wind passes over it, and it is
gone, and its place knows it no more.
But the steadfast love of the LORD is from everlasting to
everlasting on those who fear him, and his righteousness
to children's children, to those who keep his covenant and
remember to do his commandments.
The LORD has established his throne in the heavens, and
his kingdom rules over all.
Psalm 103:15-19 (ESV)*

*The just man walketh in his integrity: his children are
blessed after him.
Proverbs 20:7*

What a beautiful picture is painted in these verses! God designed godly families to reflect His glory to the world and to build His kingdom. Christian husbands and fathers must actively study the Bible's teaching on the family and then lead, serve, and love the family God has blessed them with. God's gift of a godly wife and children will be one of our greatest joys and most lasting legacies we leave on this earth!

Know What Biblical Marriage Is

Study Scripture:

1. For what purposes did God create marriage?

Gen. 1:27, 1:31

_____

Gen. 2:18

_____

Gen. 1:28; Ps. 127:3-5; Mal. 2:15

_____

_____

Ps. 128:1-4; Prov. 5:18, 18:22

_____

Prov. 5:15-21; 1 Cor. 7:2, 7:9

_____

Isa. 62:5; Matt. 22:2; Eph. 5:23-30; Rev. 19:7, 21:2

_____

_____

_____

2. Must all people be married?

1 Cor. 7:1, 7:7-9

_____

3. What obligations does the husband assume in the marriage covenant?

Eph. 5:25-29; Col. 3:19; 1 Pet. 3:7

_____

_____

Gen. 3:16; 1 Cor. 11:3; Eph. 5:23

_____

Deut. 24:5; 1 Tim. 5:8

_____

4. What obligations does the wife assume in the marriage covenant?

Gen. 2:18; Prov. 31:12; Eph. 5:22-24; Col. 3:18; 1 Tim. 5:14; Tit. 2:4-5; 1 Pet. 3:1

_____

_____

_____

_____

5. What are the only Biblical reasons for ending a marriage covenant?

Matt. 5:31-32, 19:3-9; Rom. 7:2-3; 1 Cor. 7:39

_____

_____

_____

6. How has Jesus loved his bride, the Church?

Rom. 5:6-8, 8:34-39; Eph. 5:25

_____

_____

7. If a husband is to imitate Jesus' love for us, should he love his wife only when he feels like it? Should he love her only when she deserves his love?

Ps. 103:10; Rom. 5:6-8; 1 Pet. 4:1; 1 John 4:7-21

_____

_____

_____

8. As a husband, how should we love our wife? If she does not submit, are we excused from the responsibility to love her? Why should we love our wives?

Eph. 5:22-33; Col. 3:19; 1 Pet. 3:7

_____

_____

_____

9. What does love do?

1 Cor. 13:1-13

_____

_____

_____

10. What does love not do?

1 Cor. 13:1-13

_____

_____

_____

_____

Examine Yourself:

1. In the traditional marriage vows, what does the husband promise to do?

2. What does the wife promise to do?

3. Do you think of love more as a feeling, or as an action?

4. Can a husband love his wife even if he doesn't see anything lovely about her?

5. Should a husband wait to love his wife only when she shows love, respect, or submission to him?

6. How can husbands imitate the sacrificial love of Christ for their wives?

7. Can you love with Christ's love by your own strength?

8. In what ways can you exercise sacrificial love for your future wife right now?

9. How are you showing love to those in your own family right now?

Hear Counsel:

- The husband is a picture of Christ to the wife. How you handle this position, as a husband, will greatly affect her and your whole family.

- The way you love your wife should imitate and picture how Jesus loves her.

- "I realized I was committing my life to this person no matter what. I was going to serve this person to make her life better and more enjoyable. I would not make any demands, just love her unselfishly – her needs would come before mine. Eventually she would do the same for me, and we both would become more unselfish" (from a Christian husband, speaking of his attitude when he entered marriage).

- Learn to understand and care for the women in your own family (your mother and sisters), as a young man, and you will have a head start on knowing your wife well.

- Don't think character problems will go away when you are married; they will be magnified. It's important to form godly habits now!

- Be prepared for big changes in your life when you are married.

- Plan and expect to spend lots of time and effort building a strong relationship with your future wife.

- Sharpen your communication skills – your marriage will rely on them!

- Have practical plans for loving your wife and spending time with her. When she has to spend all day at home with little children, she will need to interact with a mature person at the end of the day. Plan regular times to talk together and go for outings.

- Understand the gravity of marriage, and take it seriously. Study the Bible, read books, and talk to godly men to prepare yourself. Don't expect it all to just work out well without lots of effort on your part.

- Enter marriage with a strong commitment. Divorce is not an option!

- It is important to understand the roles of husband and wife, as we find them in Genesis 1 and 2 when God created man "in His image" and "very good." Man was given a calling, and he needed help. God gave Adam a wife to be his helper in his calling, all *before the fall.* Thus we see that if a man has no life direction and purpose, and if he has not submitted to God's calling for him, he is not ready for a helper. Understanding this foundational concept can help you avoid much frustration in your marriage: The husband has a calling, and the wife is to be his helper. She will have a hard time helping him if he doesn't know where he is going!

Take Action:

1. Read and summarize chapter 7, "As Christ Loved the Church," in **The Family, God's Weapon for Victory**, by Robert Andrews.

2. Read Chapter 3, "The Covenant Husband," in **Bound for Glory**, by R. C. Sproul, Junior.

3. Buy your own copy of **The Exemplary Husband**, by Stuart Scott, and read it, marking sections you think will be useful later. Keep this book to refer to later in your married years! Read "Chapter Eight, A Husband's Responsibility – Love."

4. Read chapter 4, "Love: The Labor of Christian Hedonism" and chapter 8, "Marriage: A Matrix for Christian Hedonism," in **Desiring God**, by John Piper.

5. Read **Reforming Marriage**, by Douglas Wilson, and summarize each chapter in your own words.

6. Ask your father to tell you ways that he sacrifices and shows his love for your mother.

7. List at least 25 specific ways you could show love for your wife when you are a husband. Talk about this list with your parents.

8. Evaluate how well you are loving your mother and sisters right now. How much time and energy do you sacrifice for them? Practice loving them even when you don't think they deserve it. Besides being good practice for loving a wife, we should be

loving our mothers and sisters anyway!

9. Keep up your communication skills by having regular conversations with your parents, writing letters, or by keeping a journal.

10. Thank God for loving you faithfully, even when you sin, and pray that you will be able to show that same love to your future wife someday.

For Further Study:

1. Read **The Intimate Marriage**, by R. C. Sproul.

2. Read chapter 10, "A Wife: To Love and Honor," in **Family Man, Family Leader**, by Philip Lancaster.

3. Read chapter 10, "What God Joins Together," in **Make It Your Ambition**, by John Notgrass.

4. Read **A Sacred Foundation**, by Michael Farris and L. Reed Elam.

5. Think of two or three Christian couples that you respect the most in your church, family or community. On a sheet of paper, list the things you respect most about them, and the ways you see them treating each other in a godly manner.

6. Ask these couples if you can "interview" them, and ask them questions about their marriage and what they think is crucial to understand before entering marriage.

7. See "Loving a Wife" in **Plants Grown Up**, by Pam Forster, for additional projects and studies.

Make a Habit of Family Worship

Study Scripture:

1. How is the faith to be passed on to the next generation?

Deut. 6:4-9; Ps. 71:15-19, 78:1-8, 145:4; Eccl. 12:1; Eph. 6:4; 2 Tim. 3:14-15

_____

_____

_____

_____

2. What happened to Israel when one generation failed to raise the next in the fear of the LORD?

Judg. 2:10-15

_____

_____

Examine Yourself :

1. Does your family have regular family worship?

2. Who leads this worship time?

3. Why is family worship important?

4. What elements should be included in family worship?

Hear Counsel:

- It is important to make family worship a priority and a habit. Lead in regular family worship from the very beginning of your marriage!

- Leading in family worship is a large part of being the spiritual leader in your home.

- Family worship does not have to be sophisticated, but it must be consistent!

- Family worship should include reading the Bible, praying, and singing.

Take Action:

1. Read and summarize each chapter of **Thoughts on Family Worship**, by James W. Alexander.

2. With your father's help, lead a family worship time for your family now. Consider doing this for one day each week, with your father's permission and/or help.

3. Read "Chapter 9 – The Father is a Priest: Intercessor and Worship Leader," in **Family Man, Family Leader**, by Philip Lancaster. What three basic elements of family worship are given here?

4. List at least 10 different ideas for the content of your family worship times. Plan some things you could do with just your wife, and then others that you could do with younger and older children as well. Discuss this list with your parents, and ask them for more ideas.

For Further Study:

1. List several times you could conduct regular worship in your future family's schedule.

2. For additional projects and ideas, see "Leadership: Faithfulness in Family Worship," in **Plants Grown Up**, by Pam Forster.

3. For a more complete argument in favor of family worship, see Part II, Chapter III of **A Christian Directory** by Richard Baxter (titled "Disputation, Whether the Solemn Worship of God in and by Families as Such, be of Divine Appointment").

Discipline Faithfully

Study Scripture:

1. What is one of the primary ways our children will learn from us?

Prov. 23:26

_____

2. For what reasons does God discipline us? Should we discipline our children for the same reasons?

Heb. 12:5-11; Rev. 3:19

_____

_____

3. What advice does Proverbs give to parents?

Prov. 13:24, 19:18, 22:6, 23:13-14, 29:15, 29:17

_____

_____

_____

4. Why should parents discipline their children?

Prov. 3:12, 13:24, 22:6, 22:15, 23:13-14, 23:24, 29:15, 29:17

_____

_____

_____

5. What specific problem should we guard against while disciplining? How can you do this?

Eph. 6:4; Col. 3:21

_____

_____

6. What advice does Proverbs give to children?

Prov. 1:8, 3:11, 4:1, 6:20-21, 13:1, 15:5, 23:22-26

_____

_____

_____

7. What are the benefits of listening to parents and accepting their discipline?

Prov. 1:8-9, 4:1-13, 6:20-24, 10:17, 13:18, 15:32, 23:22-25

_____

_____

_____

_____

8. What happens to those who refuse instruction?

Prov. 10:17, 13:18, 15:32, 19:27, 30:17

_____

_____

_____

9. What happened to Eli and his sons when he failed to discipline them?

1 Sam. 2-4

Examine Yourself:

1. Are you committed to taking time to discipline your future children every day?

2. Will you accept the primary responsibility of training your children, with your wife's help? Will you set standards for discipline so that she can discipline the children when you are not present?

3. Will you take time and energy to base your discipline and instruction on Scripture? Don't just yell at your kids when they do something that irritates you!

4. What are your convictions about the use of the rod?

5. Do you show impatience or a quick temper in your present relationships? How can you put off this habit so that you can patiently train your children as a father?

Hear Counsel:

- Training children in righteousness is one of the father's greatest responsibilities—the Bible says that the father who loves his son will discipline him.

- The most effective training you will ever give your children will be the example you set for them.

- Don't discipline in anger. Do it lovingly, with Scripture. You are to discipline children for their own good and for God's glory, not just because their misbehavior irritates you.

- Be both just and merciful, as God is to us.

- Know how to resolve conflicts.

- You can train children in three ways: First, train by setting an example. You should be living out the same Christian behavior that you need to teach them, and, to a great extent, they will imitate your behavior. Secondly, teach them what the Bible says about how they are to behave. You can do this through family worship, through Bible study time with them, and by taking time to explain the Scriptural reasons behind the discipline that you administer from day to day. This discipline is the third means of training, and it should include correcting disobedience and encouraging right behavior.

Take Action:

1. Read Chapters 20-23 ("Train up a Child," "Controlling the Child," "Teaching Kingdom Principles," and "Nurturing our Kingdom Posterity") in **The Family, God's Weapon for Victory**, by Robert Andrews.

2. Read chapter 5, "The Covenant Child," in **Bound for Glory**, by R. C. Sproul, Junior.

3. Read and summarize chapters 8 and 9 from **Standing on the Promises**, by Douglas Wilson.

For Further Study:

1. Read "Chapter 8 – A Father is a Prophet: Moral Teacher and Enforcer," in **Family Man, Family Leader**, by Philip Lancaster. What is God's method for reaching children's hearts? By what teaching method did Jesus reach the hearts of His disciples?

2. Think about the example you are setting now, especially to younger siblings and friends. What should you change? As a father, will you be modeling the character that you want them to imitate?

3. Study a chapter in **For Instruction in Righteousness**, by Pam Forster, on a sin that you or your family needs to overcome. See what God says about this sin, and make plans to

help you, and perhaps others in your family, repent of this sin.

4. For additional projects and ideas, see "Leadership: Justly Judging in Discipline Situations," in **Plants Grown Up**, by Pam Forster.

Commit to Christian Education

Study Scripture:

1. Who gives children to parents?

Gen. 4:1, 33:5, 48:9; Josh. 24:3; Ps. 113:9, 127:3; Isa. 8:18

_____

_____

2. Who has final responsibility for a child's training and education?

Deut. 6:6-7; Ps. 78:4-7; Prov. 1:8, 4:1, 13:1, 15:5; Isa. 38:19; Eph. 6:4

_____

_____

3. Should our children's education be religiously neutral?

Deut. 6:4-9; Prov. 20:11; Mark 10:14; Acts 2:39; 2 Cor. 10:4-5; 2 Tim 3:15; 2 John 1:4

_____

_____

4. Can any education be religiously neutral?

Matt. 12:30; Luke 16:13; Rom. 1:16-32; 1 Cor. 10:21

_____

_____

Examine Yourself:

1. If God blesses you with children, do you accept the primary responsibility of educating them, with your wife's help?

2. What method of education do you plan to use for your children?

3. What part will you play in your children's education? What part will your wife play?

4. Are you committed to training your children's hearts, or just their minds? What is the difference? How will this affect your plans for their education?

5. How were you educated? Did you attend a government school, a Christian school, or were you homeschooled?

6. What about your parents — how were they educated?

7. What advantages or shortcomings have you or your parents experienced in the methods used to educate you?

Hear Counsel:

- Your decision on this issue will have a profound impact on the lives and futures of your children and the generations to follow. Make your choice with much prayer and good counsel!

- Young Christian children are not ready to fight for survival in government schools. The early ages are a time for habit forming and foundation building, not for being sent out on their own as "missionaries."

- One of the main reasons Christian parents choose not to homeschool is that they are not equipped for it, but if young people commit to homeschooling now and begin to prepare for it, they can be well prepared for the task by the time they are parents.

- Homeschooling has many advantages for raising godly children.

- When comparing homeschooling to the classroom, the question is not merely "which is more efficient?" but also, "which is more effective?"

Take Action:

1. Read **When You Rise Up**, by R.C. Sproul, Jr., and answer the study questions I have provided for you in Appendix B.

2. Read **The Home Schooling Father**, by Michael P. Farris. List some of the father's responsibilities in a homeschooling family.

3. Read Chapter 6, "Why I Plan to Train My Children at Home," in **Make It Your Ambition**, by John Notgrass. What are his 6 reasons for committing to home education?

4. Read **The Seven Laws of Teaching**, by John Milton Gregory. He outlines the simple basics of teaching, which you should be conscious of no matter how you choose to educate your children. This is simple, sound advice! This would be a good book to read through with your wife before you begin homeschooling.

5. Ask your parents what type of schooling they think would be best for your children, and if they can offer any help or advice when the time comes to begin educating your own children.

6. Talk with other godly men and women and ask them any questions you might have about education issues. Think of people you know who are homeschooling veterans, and parents or teachers you know who are involved with a private Christian school.

7. Write a paper defending some of your views on homeschooling, Christian schools, or government schools.

8. Help tutor/homeschool your younger siblings or children in someone else's family. This not only helps to equip you, but it also blesses the family you are assisting.

For Further Study:

1. Observe families of government schooled, private schooled, and homeschooled children. What strengths and weaknesses do you see?

2. Make a list of the advantages and disadvantages of home-schooling, and think of ways you could overcome those disadvantages.

3. Make a list of the advantages and disadvantages of using a Christian school, and think of ways you could overcome those disadvantages.

4. If you have not been homeschooled yourself, find an opportunity to observe a homeschool family's school day.

5. Talk to different families about their particular routine and style of homeschooling.

6. Decide how you will pay tuition if you decide to send your children to a Christian school. If you plan on homeschooling, talk to parents who have homeschooled to get an estimate of how much money you will need to budget for school books and supplies.

7. Read chapter 7, "The Necessity of a Christian Education," in **Standing on The Promises**, by Douglas Wilson.

8. Study the legal aspects of homeschooling in **Homeschooling: The Right Choice**, by Christopher Klicka.

9. Visit the HSLDA website and study your state's homeschool laws *(http://www.hslda.org/laws/default.asp)*. Find out what benefits you might gain from membership in the HSLDA.

Set High Goals!

Study Scripture:

1. What does God promise to generations that are faithful to Him?

Deut. 7:9; Ps. 103:15-19, 112:1-2

_____

_____

_____

2. What happens to people without a vision?

Prov. 19:2, 29:18; Hos. 4:6; Matt. 9:36, 15:14

_____

3. Who leaves an inheritance for his children?

Prov. 13:22, 19:14

_____

4. What inheritances can Christians leave their children that are even better than riches?

Ps. 61:5, 119:111, 127:1; Prov. 11:4, 22:9; Eph. 1:15-23; Col. 1:9-14; Matt. 6:19-21; 1 Pet. 1:3-4

_____

_____

_____

5. What should faithful Christians do in their old age?

Ps. 22:30-31, 71:17-18, 78:1-7, 79:13

_____

_____

_____

6. How does the Bible view multiplication and large families?

Gen. 1:28, 9:1; Ps. 127:3-5

_____

_____

_____

_____

_____

7. What is one thing that will bring you honor in your old age?

Prov. 16:31, 17:6

_____

Examine Yourself:

1. What goals do you have for your future family?
2. What would you like to do better than your parents or grandparents have done?
3. What would your parents or grandparents like you to do better?
4. What goals would you like your future children to reach?

5. How will you help them accomplish these goals?

6. When you reach the end of your life and look back, what do you want to see?

7. How many children do you hope to have? Why?

8. What are your convictions about birth control?

9. What would eventually happen if every Christian family had only one child?

10. What would eventually happen if every Christian family had an average of six children? What if every other family in the world continued to have an average of 1.8 children or less?

11. What would happen if every Christian family had many children, but failed to raise them in the faith?

Hear Counsel:

- You have to know where you are going before you can lead!

- It is important to set goals, not only for yourself, but also for your descendants, because great things often take more than one lifetime to accomplish!

- Don't get lazy! Pass on and improve the blessings that you have now. History shows just how important this is.

- Having many children will bring grief, not joy, if you do not raise them to be faithful, godly children.

- By investing your time in them and training them, you can give your children and grandchildren a stronger sense of purpose than you had, and, by providing them with an inheritance, you can help them accomplish more during their lifetimes.

- Seek to instill self-replicating values into the next generation.

- Don't ignore practical considerations like money. Lots of what God commands requires money to accomplish.

- *Multigenerational vision* is a powerful tool for God's kingdom!

Some Suggested Goals for Future Generations:

- "Pray and work that you, your children, your grandchildren, and all of your descendants will be faithful to Jesus Christ forever" (from John Notgrass, in **Make It Your Ambition**).

- Raise children who are faithful to Christ and live for God's glory, even in their youth.

- Raise children who are more godly than you are.

- Raise generations who follow the Bible as the standard for all of life.

- Train young people to pray for their own future children.

- Increase your descendants' impact in the church and in the culture. Help them to take the lead, set standards, and re-claim cultural pursuits such as art and music.

- Support and take part in the Church as it impacts the culture, the government, and the arts. Build biblical benevolence ministries that will replace government support of the poor and weak.

- Increase your descendants' outreach to the world, including bringing the gospel to others, caring for orphans and widows, showing hospitality, and helping other families.

- Affect civil governments for Christ's Kingdom, encourage and raise godly leaders, encourage the proper use of God's law, and help protect the aged and the unborn.

- Reclaim education, bringing the responsibility back to the home and the church, and abolishing government-run schools.

- Make Christian education better for the next generation.

- Strengthen children and prepare them for possible hardships in the future.

- Spend more time discipling our children. Give them a solid, mature Biblical worldview before marriage.

- Raise children with a better biblical understanding of the family and the biblical roles of men and women.

- Raise sons who will be wise fathers, leading and governing themselves and their families by God's Word. Raise sons who will take seriously the responsibility of being a husband and father, who will provide for and protect those under their leadership. Train them to trust God and lead with humility and courage.

- Raise daughters who rejoice in their roles as homemakers, wives, and mothers. Train them to excel in the many skills required to be a successful homemaker.

- Help your children to gain an early vision for their vocation and the necessary training.

- Develop more Biblically-informed methods for training sons in vocation.

- Help children learn more during high-school education and start on their vocational path earlier.

- Engage young men in meaningful wage earning labor earlier in life.

- Raise children who are good servants.

- Raise children with an entrepreneurial spirit, who are prepared to accept the responsibility of leadership, management, and self-employed positions in their vocations.

- Work towards debt-free ownership of houses, businesses, and land.

- Leave inheritances of land, wealth, and businesses for your descendants.

- Save money for children and grandchildren.

- Do better at planning to leave an inheritance for the 2nd and 3rd generations.

- Have an inheritance for children, and help them in the culture war. Keeping wives at home and having lots of children costs, and we have to compete against dual incomes as the cost of living rises.

- Care for and support aging parents and grandparents.

- Grandparents: help and support your children and grandchildren!

- Keep better written history of your family! Take time to record the many instances of God's blessing, mercy, and faithfulness in your lives, and learn from the history of others. Teach your children to value this heritage.

Take Action:

1. Read **Make It Your Ambition**, by John Notgrass.

2. Read Chapter 23, "Nurturing our Kingdom Posterity," in **The Family, God's Weapon for Victory**, by Robert Andrews.

3. Read "Chapter 11 - Patriarchy Beyond the Home" and "Chapter 12 - Rebuilding — One Family at a Time," in **Family Man, Family Leader**, by Philip Lancaster.

4. Ask your parents what goals they have for you, or what they hope you will be able to do that they could not.

5. Write down some goals you would like to see your children or grandchildren reach. Make a plan to help them.

6. Make a commitment now to do all you can to raise your children to be faithful Christians. Begin praying for your future children now!

For Further Study:

1. How many children do you hope to have? Find out how many descendants you would have in five generations if you and each of your descendants have that many children.

2. Make a plan for having some amount of money saved for your children in the future. You can decide whether you want to help pay for their vocational training, help them buy property, or give them the savings as inheritance.

3. Listen to **How to Pass on Convictions to Your Children**, by S.M. Davis.

Family Vision Resources

The Christian Family:

The Family, God's Weapon for Victory, by Robert Andrews, published by Sentinel Press. *(5, 6)*
> A very practical handbook for fathers and husbands, this book is full of wise advice from Mr. Andrews, all based on Scripture and his many experiences as a husband, father, and pastor. Highly recommended!

Family Man, Family Leader, by Philip Lancaster, published by Vision Forum. *(1, 3, 6, 7,10)*
> A thorough Biblical study for a head of a household. This book will help you better imitate God's character as you lead your wife and children.

Mighty Men: The Starter's Guide to Leading Your Family, by John Crotts, published by Grace and Truth Books. *(3, 7)*
> An extremely practical, concise outline of a family leader's God-given duties. Highly recommended!

Bound For Glory, by R.C. Sproul, Jr., published by Crossway Books. *(1, 3)*
> Understand God's design for the family from the beginning of time.

Make It Your Ambition, by John Notgrass, published by the Notgrass Company. *(3)*
> This book offers solid encouragement, especially to young men and women who have a few years to go before marriage. John Notgrass will encourage you to pursue a godly vision for your future, starting now!

The Exemplary Husband, by Stuart Scott, published by Focus Publishing. *(3, 7)*
> A must-have manual for Christian husbands, this book is full of Scripture and wise counsel on nearly every responsibility and temptation that husbands face.

Reforming Marriage, by Douglas Wilson, published by Canon Press.*(1, 2, 3, 6, 7)*
Another excellent study on biblical marriage, discussing the roles of husbands and wives and common temptations. Wilson rightly shows us the importance and inescapability of husbands' responsibility and headship.

The Federal Husband, by Douglas Wilson, published by Canon Press. *(1, 2, 3, 6, 7)*
This book continues the study of husbands' headship where Reforming Marriage left off, fleshing out more Scriptural teaching and applications.

Desiring God, by John Piper, published by Multnomah Publishers. *(3, 6 and online at www.desiringgod.org)*
In this book, John Piper shows us that we glorify God best by enjoying Him. Delight in God is our Scriptural duty! This attitude greatly affects the way we view our relationships to others.

The Intimate Marriage, by R.C. Sproul, published by P&R Publishing. *(3, 7)*
An approachable study on Christian marriage, including topics like communication, husband's & wife's roles, and common problems in marriage.

A Sacred Foundation: The Importance of Strength in the Home School Marriage, by Michael Farris and L. Reed Elam, published by Loyal Publishing. *(3, 6, 7)*
Practical advice for both husbands and wives. Christian marriages must be built on a trust in God and a desire to serve each other as Christ serves us.

The Complete Husband, by Lou Priolo, published by Calvary Press. *(3)*
Another practical manual, similar to **The Exemplary Husband**. This book focuses primarily on communication and gives practical questions to help you live with your wife "according to knowledge."

The Blessed Marriage, audio message by Doug Phillips, produced by Vision Forum. *(3, 10)*

Manager of His Home, audio seminar by Steven Maxwell, produced by Managers of Their Homes. *(9)*

Building a Family That Will Stand, Conference tape series by Doug Phillips, Phil Lancaster, and John Thompson. Produced by Vision Forum. *(3, 10)*

Rediscovering the Lost Treasure of Family Worship, by Jerry Marcellino, published by Audubon Press. *(1, 3, 7)*
A short booklet explaining why and how we should restore the practice of family worship.

Thoughts on Family Worship, by James W. Alexander, published by Soli Deo Gloria Publications. *(7)*
Written by a Presbyterian pastor in the 19th century, this book is a valuable study on family worship -- its history, its influence on members of the household and on society, and the mode of conducting it.

A Full Quiver: Family Planning and the Lordship of Christ, by Rick and Jan Hess, published by the Hess Family. *(1)*
Our first-choice-resource on the topic of family planning. Examines the Bible's teaching on the topic, answers 20 common arguments against large families, and addresses many other practical concerns.

Be Fruitful and Multiply, by Nancy Campbell, published by Vision Forum. *(3, 6, 10)*
A thorough study on what the Bible says about having children.

A Checklist for Parents, by Pam Forster, published by Doorposts. *(5)*
A self-examination tool for parents, listing the duties God requires and helping evaluate our obedience to these responsibilities.

The Home Schooling Father, by Michael Farris, published by Loyal Publishing. *(1, 3)*
This practical book outlines the duties of a homeschooling father, showing what a difference you can make and how to do it.

For Instruction in Righteousness, by Pam Forster, published by Doorposts. *(5, 6)*
A topical handbook for daily biblical discipline and child-training.

Plants Grown Up and **Polished Cornerstones**, by Pam Forster, published by Doorposts. *(1, 5, 6, 7)*
These books are full of resource materials, Bible studies, and projects for training boys and girls in Christian character.

Standing on the Promises: A Handbook of Biblical Childrearing, by Douglas Wilson, published by Canon Press. *(1, 2, 3, 6)*
What the Bible says about raising Christian children.

Future Men, by Douglas Wilson, published by Canon Press. *(1, 2, 3, 5, 6, 7)*
A collection of biblical wisdom to aid parents in the difficult job of raising boys. (I have provided study questions for you in Appendix B.)

Teach them Diligently, by Lou Priolo, published by Timeless Texts. *(5, 6, 7)*
How to use Scripture to train and discipline children.

Passing the Scepter—What We Should Really Teach Our Sons, audio by James McDonald. *(1)*

Rebuilding a Culture of Virtuous Boyhood, audio message by Doug Phillips, produced by Vision Forum. *(6, 7, 10)*

How to Pass on Convictions to Your Children, by S.M. Davis, produced by Vision Forum. *(6, 10)*

What's a Girl To Do?, audio message by Doug Phillips, produced by Vision Forum. *(6, 10)*

Cathedral Building: Developing a Multi-Generational Vision, audio by James McDonald. *(1)*

Basement Tape #5, "A Conversation on Building the Kingdom," produced by the Highlands Study Center. *(8)*

Christian Education:

When You Rise Up, by R. C. Sproul Jr., published by P&R Publishing. *(1, 3, 5, 6, 8)*
This book will help you understand the foundational reasons and goals which lie behind all education. R.C. Jr. puts forth the goal of education as God requires it, and gives simple but sure directions for reaching that goal. He also answers some of the common objections to homeschooling. Highly recommended! (I have provided study questions for you in Appendix B.)

Home Schooling: the Right Choice, by Christopher Klicka, published by Broadman & Holman. *(1, 3, 6, 7)*
A great resource for better understanding homeschooling, pertinent legal issues, and the failure of America's government school system.

Excused Absence, by Douglas Wilson, published by Crux Press. *(1, 2, 3, 6)*
A solid case for distinctively Christian education. Should Christian parents really enroll their children in public schools so that they may be "salt and light"?

The Seven Laws of Teaching, by John Milton Gregory, various publishers. *(3, 6, 7)*
A concise, practical, and timeless analysis of teaching and learning for all who would teach. This booklet was first published in 1884, and is now available in many

reprints, both new and used. Compare different editions and look for an unabridged copy; some newer editions have removed the original theological references.

Safely Home, by Tom Eldredge, published by Vision Forum. *(1, 3, 6, 7, 10)*
Examines the history of education in our nation, contrasts the Greek and Hebrew philosophies of education, and gives a biblical model of education.

Basement tape #1, "Homeschooling," produced by the Highlands Study Center. *(8)*

Family Vision Notes:

_____

_____

_____

_____

_____

_____

_____

Family Vision Goals:

_____

_____

_____

_____

_____

_____

_____

_____

_____

_____

In Summary...

Review and summarize your vision!

Faith & Doctrine

1. Have you made God's glory your primary goal in life?

2. If not, what changes do you need to make?

3. In what specific ways do you desire to serve God and others in your life?

4. What do you see as your strongest life purposes and gifts?

5. Are you assured of your salvation? Explain why.

6. How would you describe your denominational affiliation and doctrinal beliefs?

7. What are you doing now to study and apply God's Word in your life?

8. Are you involved as a member of a local church body? How are you serving others in this body? Do you honor the leaders of this body?

Godly Manhood

9. Do you accept responsibility for whatever people, duties, and possessions God and other authorities have entrusted to you?

10. Are you failing in any current areas of responsibility? If so, which areas? What can you do to change?

11. Do you look for ways to serve your family and friends, or do you usually expect to be served by them?

12. Do you take the initiative to get a job done, start a conversation, etc. when needed?

13. Do you seek counsel from other Christians and pray for

wisdom when making decisions? Or do you make choices based primarily on your own feelings?

14. Do you honor the authorities God has placed in your life? Are you prepared to respectfully appeal if they ask you to do something sinful? Think about your relationship with your parents, your grandparents, your bosses or teachers, your church leaders, and the civil government.

15. What kind of example do you set for your friends and siblings? In what direction do you think you influence them? How do they influence you?

16. By God's help, can you exercise self-control over your appetites? Do you struggle with temptations to gluttony, oversleeping, or lust? Are you gaining ground, by God's help, in these struggles?

Vocation

17. What unique gifts or strengths has God given you? Have you chosen a career direction? If so, what direction have you chosen? If not, what directions are you currently considering?

18. How are you pursuing this direction now? What other training or work experience will be required before you can become established in your desired career? At what point will your work be able to provide for a family?

Finances

19. Describe your convictions on tithing and giving. What is your current giving plan?

20. Do you currently budget your earnings and spending? Outline your budget plan. Have you conducted a cost of living survey to plan your future family budget?

21. What is your current approach to saving? How much savings do you currently have, and what do you plan to use it for?

22. What is your current approach to debt? Do you have any debt? If so, what did you go into debt for? What is your plan for retiring any debts you may have?

23. Have you filed a tax return before? Describe your convictions regarding taxes.

24. What insurance do you currently have? What insurance coverage do you plan to get for your future family?

25. How much do you understand about housing and transportation? Do you currently own a car, house, or land? What is your plan for providing these things for your future family?

Dowry

26. Do you plan to give a dowry to your future wife? What goals have you set for this? What will you do if a dowry is asked of you?

Courtship

27. What are your convictions regarding dating, courtship, and engagement/betrothal? How do you see your parents being involved in your courtship? How do you see a young lady's parents being involved in a courtship?

28. What particular convictions, character qualities, and preferences are you looking for in your future wife?

Family Vision

29. Are you, by God's strength, prepared to love a wife sacrificially?

30. Are you prepared to lead your wife and children in daily family worship? What plans do you have for family worship times?

31. What are your views on child discipline? What is the role of Scripture in discipline? What do you believe about using the rod?

32. What are your convictions about education? In what way do you plan to educate the children God may give you?

33. What vision and goals do you have for your future family? How many children do you hope to have? What do you want your children to remember you for in your old age? What can you do to help your children grow up to be faithful Christians?

APPENDIX A:
RECOMMENDED SUPPLIERS

1. **Books on the Path**, 803 E Young Ave., Coeur d'Alene, ID 83814. Phone: (208) 667-3234
   Website: http://www.booksonthepath.com

2. **Canon Press**, PO Box 8729, 205 E. 5th Street, Moscow, ID 83843. Toll-free: (800) 488-2034
   Website: http://www.canonpress.org/shop

3. **Christian Book Distributors**, P.O. Box 7000, Peabody, MA 01961-7000. Toll-free: (800) 247-4784
   Website: http://www.christianbook.com

4. **Covenant Media Foundation**
   Website: http://www.cmfnow.com

5. **Doorposts**, 5905 SW Lookingglass Dr., Gaston, OR 97119. Toll-free: (888) 433-4749
   Email: orders@doorposts.net
   Website: http://www.doorposts.net

6. **Exodus Provisions**, 19146 S. Molalla Avenue, Ste. A, Oregon City, OR 97045. Toll-free: (877) 396-3870
   Email: bookmaster@exodusbooks.com
   Website: http://www.exodusbooks.com
   A very helpful bookstore and mail-order website offering thousands of books for homeschooling and Christian living. Owned and operated by friends from our church, Eli and Amanda Evans.

7. **Grace & Truth Books**, 3406 Summit Blvd., Sand Springs, OK 74063. Phone: (918) 245-1500
   Website: http://www.graceandtruthbooks.com
   Another helpful supplier and publisher of Christian family and character-building books.

8. **Highlands Study Center Store**, P.O. Box 16488, Bristol,
   VA 24209-6488. Toll-free: (877) 878-2238
   Email: info@highlandsstudycenter.org
   Website: http://www.highlandsstore.com

9. **Managers of Their Homes**, 2416 South 15th Street,
   Leavenworth, KS 66048-4110. Phone: (913) 772-0392
   Website: http://www.titus2.com

10. **Vision Forum**, 4719 Blanco Road, San Antonio, TX
    78212. Toll-free: (800) 440-0022
    Website: http://www.visionforum.com

Helpful Websites:

Amazon.com http://www.amazon.com

Christian Courtship http://www.christiancourtship.com

Crown Financial Ministries http://www.crown.org

The Council on Biblical Manhood and Womanhood
http://www.cbmw.org

Dave Ramsey http://www.daveramsey.com

Desiring God Ministries http://www.desiringgod.org

Home School Legal Defense Association
http://www.hslda.org

APPENDIX B:
STUDY QUESTIONS & FORMS

Study Questions for God At Work, by Gene Edward Veith

Chapter 1. The Christian's Calling in the World

1. How does God most often bless us?

2. Where does the word *vocation* come from?

3. What did vocation mean to most people before the Reformation?

4. How many vocations can one person have?

Chapter 2. How God Works Through Human Beings

5. The abandonment of what belief allowed Christianity to be seen as a merely internal and subjective experience, with no relevance in the real world?

6. How does God punish criminals in this world?

7. Does God work through non-Christians?

Chapter 3. The Purpose of Vocation

8. What is the believer's purpose in life, according to Ephesians 2:10?

9. What do Christians do as members of God's spiritual kingdom?

10. What do Christians do as members of God's earthly kingdom?

11. Why are all vocations equal before God?

12. According to Luther, what serves God and what serves people?

13. What, then, is the purpose of vocation?

14. Is self-sufficiency possible?

15. How can we serve Christ here on earth?

Chapter 4. Finding Your Vocations

16. Are we free to choose our callings?

17. Where do our callings come from?

18. What callings do you have that you can be faithful in right now?

Chapter 5. Your Calling as a Worker

19. What callings did God give man before the Fall?

20. What does our work imitate?

21. Did God remove any of man's callings after the Fall?

22. What did God do?

23. What does the Sabbath remind us of?

24. In what way should employees relate to their masters?

25. Who do masters derive their authority from?

26. How should masters treat servants?

Chapter 6. Your Calling in the Family

27. What is the most basic of all vocations?

28. How can husbands and wives fulfill their callings?

29. More specifically, what are some ways that a husband fulfills this calling in the relationship with his wife?

30. What is included in the vocation of parenthood?

31. What is included in the vocation of childhood?

32. Is authority the primary focus of these vocations? If not, what is the primary focus?

Chapter 7. Your Calling as a Citizen

33. What are some ways you can fulfill your calling as a citizen?

34. According to the reformers, is the civil use of God's Law meant for all men, or for Christians only?

35. How are we to relate to earthly governments, according to Romans 13?

36. How can civil rulers sin against their vocation?

37. When is it right to disobey a civil ruler?

Chapter 8. Your Calling in the Church

38. Why is the institutional church important?

39. What are the specific callings of pastors?

40. How is the idea of "spiritual gifts" best understood?

Chapter 9. The Ethics of Vocation

41. How much of our lives involves vocation?

42. How does understanding vocation help us discern between good works and sin?

43. Can we sin by doing something that someone else is rightly called to do?

44. What are the results of acting outside of our vocation?

Chapter 10. Bearing the Cross in Vocation

45. What sort of trials can we experience in our vocations?

46. How does the Devil want us to view our vocations?

47. How should we view them instead?

48. How should we respond to trials in vocation?

49. Why can we relax and pursue our vocations with confidence?

Chapter 11. Conclusion: Resting in Vocation

50. What will happen if Christians can recover the doctrine of

vocation?

51. Where do our callings come from?

52. How can we also find rest in vocation?

Questions for *Future Men*, by Douglas Wilson

Chapter 1. The Shape of Masculinity

1. According to Douglas Jones, how can we think of masculinity?

2. What does it mean for men (and boys) to be lords?

3. What does it mean to be husbandmen?

4. What does it mean to be saviors?

5. What does it mean to be sages?

6. What does it mean to be glory-bearers?

Chapter 2. Effeminacy and Biblical Masculinity

7. In what two ways can boys depart from true masculinity?

8. Why does counterfeit masculinity like to make excuses?

9. How are we to avoid the extremes of counterfeit masculinity?

Chapter 3. A Call for Fathers

10. How should wise fathers discipline their sons?

11. Does the cultural mandate of Genesis still apply to us?

12. What are a few ways we fulfill this mandate?

13. When should boys begin learning to be good husbands?

14. What is the central duty of husbands in marriage?

15. What is the central duty of wives?

Chapter 4. A Covenant Home

16. When does the obligation to fear and serve God begin?

17. What is a covenant?

18. Should we view the biblical covenants as separate and chang-

ing, or as related and building on one another?

19. When do sons born in a believing home become part of the covenant?

20. What temptations are common to those within the covenant?

21. What type of young men does the author refer to as "thunder puppies"? In what way do they sin?

Chapter 5. Doctrinal Meat

22. What particular exhortation is given to young men in Titus 2?

23. What character qualities does this exhortation encompass?

24. What is meant by a true "Christian worldview"?

25. What is the gospel?

26. As young men gain a solid grasp on a Christian worldview, what two issues are particularly important?

27. What is the true meaning of "meekness"?

28. What did Jesus promise to the meek?

29. What is the earthly mission of the church?

Chapter 6. Secret Sin, Tolerated Sin

30. How will hidden sin affect you?

31. How will hidden sin affect others?

32. What kind of open sin is often tolerated in the home?

Chapter 7. Laziness and Hard Labor

33. What were we created for?

34. Why is work hard?

35. What kind of life comes to a boy who has a habit of laziness?

36. What is the foundation of a biblical work ethic?

37. What are the characteristics of laziness?

38. Does being lazy make life easier?

Chapter 8. Money Paths and Traps

39. Is wealth good, or bad?

40. What three principles does God give regarding the acquisition of wealth?

41. What is more important than wealth?

42. In what ways do young men commonly throw their wealth away?

Chapter 9. Christian Liberty

43. Christian liberty frees us *from* what?

44. Christian liberty frees us *to* what?

45. What is the purpose of Christian liberty?

46. What should parents ask sons when a disagreement arises over a matter of Christian liberty?

47. Is the purpose of Christian liberty being accomplished if a young man uses this liberty to please himself?

Chapter 10. Mom and Sisters

48. How should fathers teach sons to honor their future wives?

49. Why should men teach their wives about disciplining their sons?

50. What kind of emotional closeness in the family will bring trouble later on?

51. What three things must mothers do to encourage toughness as they train their sons?

52. How and why should boys be taught manners?

Chapter 11. Church and Worship

53. Should the fruit of the Spirit be manifested in both men and women?

54. Will these character qualities appear differently in men and women?

55. How is worship often improperly feminized?

56. What is properly masculine worship?

57. Should children be included in worship?

58. What does a young man need to learn about wise participation in worship?

Chapter 12. Giants, Dragons, and Books

59. How does reading other books affect how we read the Bible?

60. Are fictional stories naturally unbiblical?

61. Why are so many fictional stories good for us to read?

Chapter 13. School Work

62. What threat do traditional schools pose to masculinity?

63. How can this be (at least partially) avoided?

64. What danger should homeschooled young men guard against?

65. How should this be avoided?

Chapter 14. Friends

66. What kind of friends should young men avoid?

67. What is friendship defined by (for both parties)?

68. How does proper friendship prepare you to be a good husband?

69. How can parents protect their children from unhealthy friendships?

Chapter 15. Fighting, Sports, and Competition

70. Why should boys learn when, where, and how to fight?

71. When is it right to fight?

72. What must boys learn in playing war?

73. Are sports lawful?

74. What temptations must we guard against while enjoying sports?

Chapter 16. Girls and Sex

75. How can young men best learn to honor and respect girls and women?

76. What will be likely to happen to young men who do not habitually honor girls and women?

77. Where does our sin come from?

78. Where can we find true purity?

79. What do young men most need in order to combat temptations to sexual sin?

80. What should parents pray for regularly?

81. What is happening to young men who allow themselves to listen to or watch the average modern music and entertainment?

82. Whom must emotionally needy girls be protected from most?

83. Why does the Christian faith say *no* to the sexual urges of young men?

Chapter 17. Courtship and Betrothal

84. How should the parents of a young lady be involved in her courtship?

85. How should the parents of a young man be involved in his courtship?

86. There is nothing magical about the words "courtship" or "betrothal"; we must live before God with _____ and be governed by _____.

87. What key principles should a young man remember as he approaches courtship?

88. What kind of women should young men avoid?

89. In contrast, what are the characteristics of a godly woman?

90. Which parents do young people do well to observe when considering a future spouse?

91. What kind of young man should you want to be?

Chapter 18. Contempt for the Cool

92. More than just reacting against popular culture, what should parents teach their children to do?

93. How can the concept of "cool" replace the Word of God?

94. What key principles should sons be instructed in where pop culture is concerned?

95. What important factor must be considered when we are evaluating the lawfulness or sinfulness of something?

96. What question should we learn to ask about cultural trends?

97. Why is pop culture actually an anti-culture?

Conclusion. Fighting Idols

98. What kind of false gods are harder for us to identify?

99. What are some common false gods that tempt us today?

100. What is the difference between the wise man and the foolish man in Jesus' parable? What did they have in common?

101. How do young men sometimes tend to prepare for marriage? How should they prepare instead?

102. How should young men see the war we are involved in?

Appendix A. Liberty and Marijuana

103. Biblically speaking, what is sinful about taking drugs?

104. What are the 5 good uses of wine given in the Bible?

105. How can the use of wine or tobacco differ from the use of drugs?

Appendix B. *Proverbs* Was Written for Boys

106. What is one theme that comes up repeatedly in Proverbs?

107. Why must parents discipline boys?

108. What specific instruction does Proverbs say parents should give their sons?

Study Questions for *Sex Is Not the Problem (Lust Is)* (first released as *Not Even a Hint*), by Joshua Harris

1. After reading this book, what would you say is the definition of lust?

2. In what 3 areas are we often misguided in our battle with lust?

3. What is the proper godly attitude towards sex?

4. What happens if we base our battle with lust on legalism?

5. What is the difference between justification and sanctification?

6. God has created men and women with different and complimentary desires. How is this designed to glorify Him? How does lust twist these differences and use them sinfully?

7. What is the "God-centered" view of sex?

8. Do you need to cut back on your "media intake"?

9. Why is accountability important?

10. Why is it important to be part of a local church?

11. What common mistakes should we guard against in our accountability?

12. What is the only weapon with which you can successfully fight lust?

13. What Scriptures have you memorized that you can use to combat lust? Are there others that you can memorize to help you fight in a specific area of temptation?

14. How can you "sow to the Spirit" in your life right now?

15. Rather than becoming preoccupied with overcoming lust, what should you focus on?

Study Questions for God's Design for Scriptural Romance, by John Thompson

This series of articles by John Thompson is a very thorough study of courtship principles as we find them in the Bible. Each article looks into these biblical principles and suggests applications to our courtships today. Thompson lays a strong foundation of godly principles, although not every courtship needs to apply these principles exactly as he recommends. (See notes after some questions for several additional perspectives). Overall, this series is very helpful in stimulating thought and in discussing the various biblical principles involved in courtship.

At the time I am writing, Thompson's work is not yet available in book form, but you can read and print these articles online at *www.christiancourtship.com*. Information on a printed edition should be posted there if a book becomes available.

Chapter 1. Rediscovering Timeless Truths

1. What does Thompson mean by betrothal?

2. How would you define "betrothal"? How would you define "engagement"? Do you see a difference between the two terms? Which term would you rather use?

3. List the five reasons Thompson believes that betrothal is transcultural. Do you agree?

4. What does Thompson mean by each of the following principles for godly romance?

   Piety
   Patriarchy
   Purity
   Preparedness
   Patience

Chapter 2. Dealing With the Dating Dilemma

5. Where did dating come from historically?

6. What changes in the 20th century contributed to the dating problem today?

7. List some ways parents and young people can resist the dating spirit.

Chapter 3. Preparing Your Children for Biblical Betrothal

8. How does the author define courtship?

9. How does he define betrothal?

10. List some ways parents can prepare their children for godly courtship and betrothal.

Chapter 4. Choosing a Spouse by Faith, not Feelings

11. Which of Thompson's three men are you most like in your views?

12. Give honest answers to the 5 true/false questions Thompson asks before you read beyond them for his answers.

13. Describe God's moral will.

14. Describe God's sovereign will.

15. Describe the idea of God's individual will and how we know it.

16. Do you believe that God reveals His will to us through inner prompts, voices, or feelings?

17. How can you tell the difference between God revealing His will and your own feelings and temptations?

18. If another Christian tells you "God told me it is His will for you to marry so-and-so, how will you know if he is lying?

19. How should we respond to God's sovereign will?

20. How should we respond to God's moral will?

21. When do we know for certain who we are meant to marry?

Chapter 5. Talking Biblically about Feelings

22. In what four ways do we use the word "feeling"?

23. Which uses of this word are accurate and biblical?

24. Which uses of this word are unbiblical and often sinful?

Chapter 6. How to Marry – The Friendship Stage

25. Young men: Considering your gifts and circumstances, do you think you should be married, or stay single? Do your parents agree with your view?

26. List three reasons someone should remain single.

27. Should a Christian ever marry a non-believer? Why?

28. What kind of love is present in the friendship stage?

29. How can we apply piety in the friendship stage?

30. Although it is not discussed in this article, prayer should play an important part in each of these four stages. How do you think we should pray during the friendship stage?

31. How can we apply patriarchy in the friendship stage?

32. How can we apply purity in the friendship stage?

33. How can we apply preparedness in the friendship stage?

34. How can we apply patience in the friendship stage?

Chapter 7. How to Marry – The Courtship Stage

35. What five goals (from the friendship stage) must be met before entering the courtship stage?

36. What is the basic purpose of the courtship stage?

37. Name three ways that God gives you wisdom for choosing a spouse.

38. How can we apply piety in the courtship stage?

39. What do you think we should pray for during the courtship stage?

40. Should we compare convictions during this stage?

41. Should we compare preferences during this stage?

42. How can we apply patriarchy in the courtship stage?

Note: You may find this section a bit unusual. Read other authors for a wider perspective on parental involvement in finding potential spouses. Thompson seems to encourage parents to take the initiative in spouse selection, conducting inquiries as to the suitableness of potential spouses without their children's knowledge. Should a young man's father really be initiating such inquiries for him? Should a father express interest to young men or their parents as a way of finding potential husbands for his daughters? What do you think?

Parents should be deeply involved in observing, pointing out, and evaluating possible spouses for their children, but I agree more with the perspective of Wilson and Andrews -- young men need to be the initiators from the beginning of a courtship. This is a prime opportunity for a young man to set a precedent of manly leadership for the rest of their future marriage, should the courtship so result. If fathers conduct too much of the initial investigation, or initiate conversations about possible matches with others apart from their son's involvement, they are robbing him of this opportunity to grow in manhood and accept the risks involved in such initiation. Should young men seek the counsel and oversight of their parents before selecting a potential wife or initiating a courtship? Absolutely!

43. How can we apply purity in the courtship stage?

*Note: At first, our family was surprised by what Thompson says about emotions during the courtship phase. After going through my sister's courtship, we are convinced that certain emotions cannot be avoided during the courtship period! What Thompson is saying, however, is that we should avoid **emotional bonding** during this time, which is true. Courtship is a time of evaluation, and commitments have not yet been made. Since the relationship is not bound* *by a covenant, and may still be broken off, those involved should keep this in mind and continue to guard their own (and each other's) emotions, remaining emotionally pure for their future spouse, who may yet be out of the picture.*

44. How can we apply preparedness in the courtship stage?

45. How can we apply patience in the courtship stage?

Chapter 8. How to Marry: Courtship Questions

46. What should we follow – our parents' courtship example, or God's courtship principles?

47. Where is the proper place for romance in the Biblical courtship model?

48. In what ways should a young man's father be involved in his courtship? *Note: See comments on parental involvement on the previous page.*

49. Beyond immediate family, who else should be consulted when evaluating a potential spouse?

50. Give three reasons why you should examine a potential spouse's family during the courtship stage.

51. Young men or young women: name some godly relatives or other wise persons who could guide you through courtship if your parents are unsaved, unwilling, or unavailable.

52. When would it be appropriate to marry against your father's wishes?

53. What problems are likely to arise when sons or daughters attempt to practice courtship while away from the home?

54. How can you avoid or overcome these problems?

55. List four problems that can arise within a courtship when the families are separated by a great distance.

56. How can you avoid or overcome these problems?

57. Do older, more mature singles need to follow courtship principles?

58. How can you begin following God's principles for romance if you have already been involved in dating?

59. How long should the courtship stage last?

60. Could you give answers to the list of inquiry questions that Thompson provides?

61. How do you think someone else would answer them if they were describing you?

Chapter 9. How to Marry: The Betrothal Stage

62. What are four reasons the betrothal stage is important?

63. What is the author's definition of betrothal?

64. In what ways can we apply piety in the betrothal stage?

65. How might we pray during the betrothal stage?

66. How should the father of a daughter apply patriarchy in the betrothal stage?

67. How can we apply purity in the betrothal stage?

68. In what two ways might we apply preparedness in the betrothal stage?

69. What three goals does the biblical bride-price accomplish?

70. In what other ways could we meet these same goals?

Note: In **Tools of Dominion,** *Gary North further discusses the biblical bride price and how we should apply it today. He writes that the bride price and dowry are no longer* **required** *by Scripture, except possibly as a criminal penalty. Ideally, the purposes of the Old Testament bride price are now accomplished through the church and civil government: 1. Baptism and church membership now serve as a screening device and as evidence of membership in the family of God's people. 2. Other economic and legal contracts are now available to provide the protective functions originally provided by the bride price. 3. The church-wide practice of monogamy also protects against several problems that the bride price addressed in a polygamist culture.*

Safeguards like the bride price may have extra value for families practicing courtship in a small home-church setting or in isolation from church authority and the broader Christian community. However, if Christian families practice courtship and betrothal in submission to godly authorities in the family and church, remaining accountable to the Christian community around them, the bride price becomes less necessary.

*All this to say — the Bible does not say we **must** continue giving a dowry or bride price, but we must still understand and apply the principles rightly.*

71. What is the difference between betrothal and engagement?

72. If a dowry is given, when do you think it should be transferred? At the point of betrothal/engagement? During the wedding? After the wedding?

73. How can we apply patience in the betrothal stage?

Chapter 10. How to Marry: The Wedding Stage

74. How can we apply piety in the wedding stage?

75. What should we pray for in the wedding stage?

76. What three things does God intend for marriage to be?

77. How can we apply preparedness in the wedding stage?

78. What are the three parts of a biblical wedding?

79. How can we apply patriarchy in the wedding stage?

80. In Scripture, who traditionally plans and finances the wedding?

81. Who plans and finances the wedding in today's culture?

82. Who officiates at weddings in Scripture?

Note: The Bible doesn't actually say much about who officiates at weddings. Thompson points out that weddings in the Bible typically take place in the home of the groom. He also suggests that weddings in the Bible are officiated by the parents, and that the only function of the church is that of witnessing the marriage. In contrast, Gary North (again, in **Tools of Dominion**) says this authority for approving marriages has shifted from the family to the church. The institutional focus is now on God's Kingdom and the Church, Christ's bride, rather than on a specific family line, as it was in the Old Testament.

83. Do you think it is wrong for a pastor or elder to officiate at a wedding? Why or why not?

84. Do you think it is wrong for the father of the bride or groom to perform the wedding? Why or why not?

85. What is the biblical role of the church in a Christian wedding?

86. What is the biblical role of the civil government in a Christian wedding?

87. Does the state really have authority to forbid or authorize marriages?

88. How can we apply purity in the wedding stage?

89. How can we apply patience in the wedding stage?

Study Questions for When You Rise Up, by R. C. Sproul, Junior.

Chapter 1. The Goal of Education

1. Why is it important to approach the education issue with a clear mind?

2. What three things are the major "battlefields" in the education "war"?

3. What three questions should we answer before trying to address the above issues?

4. Why does R. L. Dabney say that education is a spiritual process?

5. Biblically speaking, how should we define the goal of education?

6. What two things should we most want for our children?

7. If we begin with the Bible, how should we rightly teach various other subjects (like math)?

8. We must teach our children to love, trust, and obey God, and what else?

9. What question should we ask even before we ask what education is for?

10. What is the true goal and purpose of education?

Chapter 2. Parents: God's Chosen Teachers

11. What are two reasons that character is not taught in state schools?

12. According to R. L. Dabney, what is the difference between "education" and "dexterity"?

13. Why is the notion of neutrality in education a scam?

14. How can you tell if God has equipped you to homeschool?

15. What is the major problem with the "factory model" that state schools follow?

16. What do parents promise in baptismal vows?

Chapter 3. You Shall Speak of Them

17. What does "worldliness" mean?

18. What does "faith" mean?

19. Why should the Bible be valuable to us?

20. Why did God give us the Bible?

21. What method does God tell us to use in training our children?

22. How did Jesus teach while He was on earth?

Chapter 4. The Three G's

23. Can parents provide a godly education by merely replacing or reacting to the content taught by government schools?

24. What desire do Christian parents and parents from other religions hold in common? On what particular point of this issue should we disagree?

25. What wrong motivation is often behind our homeschooling efforts?

26. In Deuteronomy, what does Moses describe as the "good life"?

27. What are the "Three G's"?

Chapter 5. Boys and Girls

28. Why should we teach boys and girls differently?

29. What is meant by "antithesis"?

30. What is one of Satan's greatest weapons in this war?

31. Why do children often miss the importance of the antithesis?

32. Understanding the antithesis may frighten our children. How

should we help avoid that fear?

33. What specific principles should we emphasize in our daughters' training?

34. What specific principles should we emphasize in our sons' training?

Chapter 6. Objections Answered

35. Rather than rational arguments, what problem generally leads homeschoolers to quit?

36. At least 9 objections are mentioned and disputed in this chapter. Name each objection, and describe why it is invalid.

A Concluding Unscientific Postscript

37. What is truly needed in order to raise godly children as described in this book?

Career Choice Evaluation Sheet

Name: _____ Date: _____

Career Direction: _____

1. Describe this career. What work would you be doing? What responsibilities might you have? Who might you be working for? What work hours would be required? How would you receive income?

   _____

   _____

   _____

   _____

2. Will this career path help you do better at your other important callings, or will it hinder them? Will it:

   A. Glorify God and advance Christ's kingdom? _____

   B. Serve others by offering a useful service or product? _____

   C. Provide enough money for your family to live on? _____

   D. Allow you enough time at home and with your family? _____

   E. Keep you from unnecessary temptations to sin? _____

3. Would you have the blessing of your parents in choosing this path?

   _____

4. Would you have the encouragement of other friends, family, and other godly men?

   _____

5. Does this work make use of the unique gifts and abilities God has given you?

   _____

6. Is this career possible to attain in light of your abilities, situation, and finances?

_____

7. Have you spent any time doing this work, to see if it fits your personality and gifts?

_____

8. Is it something you enjoy doing? Does this work bring satisfaction?

_____

9. Do you have any training in this area already?

_____

10. Can you get the necessary education and training that you still need for this work?

_____

11. Would this direction allow for growth and increase of skills and salary?

_____

12. Could you eventually train sons or other young people in this same direction?

_____

13. Does this career require any special degrees, certification, or licenses?

_____

14. What could you do to pursue this career direction?

_____

_____

_____

_____

Cost of Living Survey

Date: _____ Location: _____

Housing:

Mortgage or rent	$_____
Electricity	$_____
Gas (if applicable)	$_____
Water	$_____
Phone	$_____
Other (garbage, etc.)	$_____
Maintenance (if buying)	$_____

Auto:

Gas & Oil	$_____
Repair/maintenance	$_____
Replacement	$_____

Insurance:

Renter's/homeowner's	$_____
Auto	$_____
Life	$_____
Medical	$_____
Other _____	$_____

Food	$_____
Clothing	$_____
Household/Misc.	$_____
Savings	$_____
Medical/Dental	$_____
Entertainment/Hospitality	$_____
Gifts	$_____
Charity/Missions	$_____
Tithe	$_____
Other _____	$_____
Other _____	$_____
Total Cost of Living:	$_____

Budget Chart

Time period: _____

Wages: $_____

Interest: $_____

Other income: $_____

Total: $_____

Less taxes: $ - _____

Total income for this period: $_____

Budget Item:	Amount Spent:	% of Total:
_____	$_____	_____%
_____	$_____	_____%
_____	$_____	_____%
_____	$_____	_____%
_____	$_____	_____%
_____	$_____	_____%
_____	$_____	_____%
_____	$_____	_____%
_____	$_____	_____%
_____	$_____	_____%
_____	$_____	_____%
_____	$_____	_____%
_____	$_____	_____%
_____	$_____	_____%
_____	$_____	_____%
Totals (check):	$_____	_____%

Essential Tool List

1. **Cordless drill/screwdriver** – A timesaver for most projects in the house or outdoors.
2. **Ratchet/Socket set** (With 1/4", 3/8", and 1/2" heads and extension) – Auto repair.
3. **Wrench set** (open end/box) – Auto/bike repair.
4. **Crescent wrench** – Auto/bike repair.
5. **Vice Grips or Channel Lock pliers** – Auto repair, plumbing, opening tough lids.
6. **Needlenose Pliers** – For doing anything with wire, and lots of home projects.
7. **Wire cutter pliers**
8. **Claw hammer**
9. **Screwdriver with changeable bits** – A handy tool for around the house and car.
10. **Regular flat and Phillips-head screwdrivers** – For everyday repairs and prying
11. **Pry bar** – For heavy prying.
12. **Tape measure**
13. **1-foot level** – Works great around the house and for outdoor projects — wives like things to be level!
14. **Allen wrench set** – You may need this for some auto and appliance repairs.
15. **Volt meter** – Good for checking batteries, especially on your car. Also tests electrical continuity.
16. **Assorted nails and screws** – For building and repairing things indoors and out.

ABOUT THE AUTHOR

Daniel Forster is the eldest son of John and Pam Forster, Doorposts' founders. He graduated from his homeschool education in 2002. He has worked with his parents at Doorposts since they started the business in 1990, and he is currently the office manager.

Daniel wrote **Prepare Thy Work** over the course of three years while living with his parents and working for Doorposts. With his family, he attends Reformation Covenant Church in Oregon City, Oregon.

Besides writing and working for Doorposts, Daniel enjoys spending time with his family, playing and teaching old-time fiddle, reading, photography, working outdoors, making Civil War uniforms for reenactors, and raising chickens.